Russel Wright

Joe Keller
&
David Ross

Schiffer Publishing Ltd

4880 Lower Valley Road Atglen, PA 19310 USA

Dedication

This book is dedicated to Carmen Brady and Pierre Allaud for their passion and enthusiasm for all things Russel Wright.

Library of Congress Cataloging-in-Publication Data

Keller, Joe.
Russel Wright / Joe Keller & David Ross.
p. cm.
ISBN 0-7643-1162-X
1. Wright, Russel, 1904-1976--Catalogs. 2. Tableware--United States--Collectors and collecting. 3. Tableware--United States--History--20th century. I. Ross, David, 1962- II. Title.
NK8725.5.W75 A4   2000
745'.092--dc21
00-009149

Designed by Bonnie M. Hensley
Type set in Geometr231 Hv Bt/Zurich

ISBN: 0-7643-1162-X
Printed in China
1 2 3 4

Published by Schiffer Publishing Ltd.
4880 Lower Valley Road
Atglen, PA 19310
Phone: (610) 593-1777; Fax: (610) 593-2002
E-mail: Schifferbk@aol.com
Please visit our web site catalog at **www.schifferbooks.com**

In Europe, Schiffer books are distributed by Bushwood Books
6 Marksbury Avenue Kew Gardens
Surrey TW9 4JF England
Phone: 44 (0) 20-8392-8585; Fax: 44 (0) 20-8392-9876
E-mail: Bushwd@aol.com
Free postage in the UK. Europe: air mail at cost.

This book may be purchased from the publisher.
Include $3.95 for shipping. Please try your bookstore first.
We are always looking for people to write books on new and related subjects.
If you have an idea for a book please contact us at the top address.
You may write for a free catalog.

Contents

Acknowledgments

We would like to thank the many people who assisted us in writing this book. The staff at Schiffer Publishing was supportive and helpful. Douglas Congdon-Martin helped coordinate photo shoots and oversaw the entire process. Bruce Waters can be commended for all his hard work and enthusiasm during the marathon photo shoot in California. In addition to shooting roll after roll of film, Bruce was extremely helpful with coming up with inventive ways to arrange the never ending parade of dinnerware we placed in front of his camera's lens. We are once again grateful for the contributions of Blair Loughrey. He is a rare talent that brings so much to "Team Schiffer". Thanks also to Donna S. Baker for her help with the photo shoot in Atglen, PA, and Molly Higgins for editing.

We are also very grateful to Joe Keller, Sr. for his help and generosity with the Yamato Theme Formal and Theme Informal dinnerware lines.

The staff of Syracuse University Library Special Collections was very cooperative in accessing the Russel Wright files for our research.

Bill Burke was most generous with the loan of his collection of Russel & Mary Wright's Sovereign dinnerware. Dennis Mykytyn shared his wealth of knowledge and his incredible Russel Wright Bauer collection with us. Thanks go to Dennis & Eve Mykytyn for their gracious hospitality as well.

Thank you to Michael Pratt for his help with the Iroquois chart. The support and help from Ed Kitchen during the photo shoot in Santa Monica was wonderful. Ed is a rare gem and his kindness and help made the long days of work much more pleasant. Ed was also responsible for supplying us with the incredible flowers that were grown by William "Smokey" Smith. Special thanks also to Winfield and Ruthie Foley and Scott Differ for their ongoing support.

We are most grateful for the kindness and generosity of Carmen Brady and Pierre Allaud. Carmen and Pierre have passionately collected and enjoyed Russel Wright designs for many years. They allowed unlimited access to anything we needed for photographs and Carmen's input during the photo shoot in Santa Monica was invaluable. After long days of gathering and arranging dinnerware, Carmen would somehow come up with new ideas to display it in a new and imaginative way. In addition to all of this, Carmen was an incredibly generous host during the photo shoot of her and Pierre's collection. We will be forever grateful for their warmth and friendship.

A special thank you is due the late Jean Hutchison. Jean and her husband worked at the Steubenville Pottery Company for many years. She kindly shared her many memories of the last days of operation at The Steubenville Pottery Company. We will never forget Jean's wit and smile and were honored to have known her.

Foreword

This book was written to help identify Russel Wright's dinnerware and other designs, and to present a guide to their value. It is not intended to be a biography of the artist or a comprehensive history of his designs. We heavily relied on the work of Ann Kerr and William Hennessey and strongly recommend their books for a more broad knowledge of Russel Wright.

We have chosen to address in detail Russel Wright's dinnerware, especially his American Modern and Casual China. We have provided values for each color of these lines. We have also attempted to illustrate how the variety of colors and forms work together to enhance the beauty of individual designs.

Russel Wright's designs are both collected and used. Years after being designed and produced, new enthusiasts are constantly discovering Russel Wright's creations. We hope this book, by presenting the incredible variety of Russel Wright's designs, encourages and supports the collecting and use of his dinnerware.

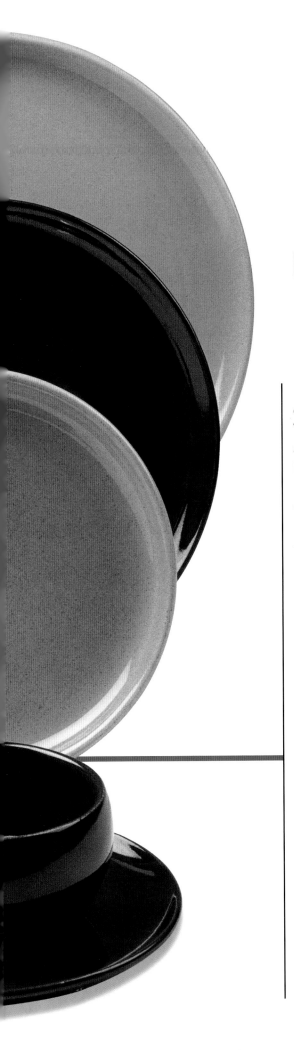

Pricing

Determining value for Russel Wright's designs has been difficult because of the wide difference in regional pricing. Russel Wright sells well in big cities—New York, San Francisco, Boston, and Atlanta—and not as well in middle America. The Internet has helped to even out values, but also causes aberrations.

We have attempted to take an average value—what we would expect an item to sell for by a retail dealer specializing in such products. Prices listed are for pieces free from any damage—cracks, chips, crazing, or scratches. Prices listed are for first-quality pieces. Pieces with large glaze skips or blemishes are worth considerably less than prices listed. Most pottery companies sold second-quality pieces at a reduced price. Iroquois was especially known for unloading thousands of seconds at greatly reduced prices. These items are frequently fine to use, but are not valued highly by collectors.

We have supplied price charts for Iroquois and American Modern by color. These charts list prices for known pieces. We have put "n/a" to indicate that we believe that piece to be not available—not having been produced. We have put "???" when we do not specifically know of a piece existing. Usually this means that the piece could have been produced but no examples have been brought to our attention. Please let us know if you have any of these pieces.

Prices for high-end Russel Wright have skyrocketed lately. On-line auctions, like eBay™, have allowed pieces to reach record levels. Yet, these prices cannot always be sustained. Just because a White Iroquois chop plate sells for $300 one day, does not mean it ever will again! On the other hand, several rare aqua pieces have been consistently selling for over $2000.

As with any collectible, prices ultimately must be established by individual collectors and dealers. The prices in this book should only be used as a guide.

Russel and Mary Wright

Introduction

For more than four decades, Russel Wright created designs that influenced and reflected American domestic life. From his popular and well-known dinnerware to furniture, from linoleum to fabric, from lighting to door chimes, Russel Wright's designs have become integral to our concept of the modern home.

Russel Wright was born in Lebanon, Ohio, on April 3, 1904. He attended but did not graduate from Princeton, where he worked with their student theatre group, the Triangle Players. Leaving college, Russel Wright moved to New York where he apprenticed with the successful theatre and industrial designer, Norman Bel Geddes.

In 1927, Russel Wright married Mary Einstein. Mary would be an important influence and source of support during his career. Her own designs and their collaboration on both dinnerware and their book, *Guide to Easier Living* (1951), profoundly influenced Russel's work. Mary was also a guiding force in the financial side of Russel Wright's business.

Russel Wright's work has a unique place in the history of designer items. While the pairing of a designer's name with a product is not unique, Russel Wright took such designer recognition to a new level. It was no accident that his signature is larger than

Two editions of *Guide to Easier Living*.

any other text on the backstamp of most of his designs. Russel Wright sold his name with the product. This meant that he wanted a certain level of quality for his products—a level that the demands of postwar industry could rarely accomplish to his satisfaction.

Russel was also concerned with the marketing of his designs. His attempts to advertise and distribute his own products were a constant tension with the companies who produced them. On the one hand, because they were selling the name along with the product, Russel Wright's involvement in marketing was essential. But, on the other hand, Russel Wright was an artist whose high standards were often unrealistic. His archives at Syracuse University contain hundreds of letters from a dissatisfied Wright demanding some change in a product, the marketing of a product, or the distribution of the product. Unfortunately, while his acrimonious letters sometimes improved the product or its chance of reaching the public, they just as often severed relationships with company officials who saw his intrusions into their business as unacceptable. Fortunately for Wright, most of his designs sold. Company officials would placate him as long as they were making money.

Wright's early commercial designs used spun aluminum and chrome. Working in his own studio and for Chase Brass and Copper Company, Wright produced a group of household items well ahead of their time. While spun aluminum would become extremely popular in the late 1940s and early 1950s, Wright was producing it in the early 1930s. Incorporating rattan, bamboo, and brass into his designs, he created an extremely large line of beverage sets, serving bowls, storage containers, and vases.

By the mid-1930s, Wright was designing furniture for Heywood-Wakefield and Conant Ball, and lamps

Russel Wright dinnerware and pottery.

Whoozoo the seal. From Circus Animal collection.

for a variety of companies. His American Modern line of furniture began an interest in creating uniquely American design for many aspects of home life. Making American life easier became a central goal that would permeate his work for the next decade. In the *Guide to Easier Living*, Mary and Russel wrote,

> All over America we build and furnish our homes, and live in them, as though there were retinues of servants to do the work...Certainly more than a few of today's frustrations and guilt complexes have their roots in the struggle to fit our twentieth-century selves into an eighteenth-century corset.

This interest in making life easier is seen in his first full-scale dinnerware line, also called American Modern. It was designed in 1938 and produced by Steubenville Pottery the following year. It was this dinnerware, more than anything else he designed, that made Russel Wright a household name. Insisting that form and function must be integrated, American Modern became the best selling dinnerware of its day, rivaled only by Fiesta™, made by Homer Laughlin China Co., for length of production and popularity.

American Modern was marketed as affordable dinnerware that could be used for all occasions. It could be purchased open

Russel Wright Harker.

stock but was also available in starter sets and specifically focused sets—like barbecue or children's sets. The line was available in ten colors and was produced for over twenty years.

Russel Wright's second design of a dinnerware line is seen in Casual China, produced by the Iroquois China Company. Learning from the shortcomings of American Modern, this line addressed the durability issues that had been raised by consumers of American Modern who found it crazed and chipped too easily. Iroquois, however, was made of different clay and fired at a higher temperature, and was guaranteed against breakage. Not only was this a clever advertising gimmick (Russel Wright was even known to have done live demonstrations at department stores), but it focused the consumer's attention on the longevity of the product. By repeatedly changing the line, adding pieces and colors, interest in the dinnerware could be sustained over the years. The consumer could add to the set and change the color palate; it wasn't necessary to get a new set of dishes.

In the late 1940s and early 1950s, Russel Wright designed dinnerware for Sterling China, Paden City, Knowles, Harker and other pottery companies. Each had limited success. With the Knowles and Harker lines, Russel Wright began incorporating pattern into his dinnerware. While at least partially motivated by the public's demand for decorated dinnerware, Russel Wright's work also chose to integrate nature into his designs. From the simple decorated clover of his Harker dinnerware to the more complex designs for Knowles, Russel Wright began an exploration of how to decorate using nature as his subject. This theme also recurs in his plastic dinnerware and later designs for Iroquois.

Russel Wright's most comprehensive design was the on-going design of his home, Dragon Rock, in Garrison, NY. This is where theory met with practice. From the beautiful trails surrounding his home, to the incredible detail within, Russel Wright created a comfortable living space that was part of the natural world that surrounded it. The home is also the embodiment of many of the ideas he and Mary wrote about in the *Guide to Easier Living.*

Bauer vase.

American Modern

White American Modern

American Modern was Russel Wright's first full-scale dinnerware line. Heavily advertised in New York papers early in 1939, it was released later in the year and instantly earned a place in the history of industrial design. The popularity of this design paired with its aggressive marketing campaign created a demand that was difficult for its producer, Steubenville Pottery, to satisfy.

American Modern was the first mass-produced "designer" dinnerware. While industrial designers flourished during the 1930s, most either created expensive products with limited runs or mass-produced items camouflaged by a company logo. Russel Wright, by the mid-1930s, when he was negotiating with Steubenville, was confident that the pairing of his name with a product would be beneficial to the recognition of the product in the marketplace. American Modern was targeted to middle-class affluence—to people who valued form, but were still conscious of practical function and affordability.

American Modern was a hit from the start, receiving favorable press and critical acclaim. In 1941, it won the American Designers' Institute Award for best ceramic design of the year. Numerous newspapers reviewed the product in a way reminiscent of the opening night of a Broadway show. Media hype surrounded the dinnerware line in an unprecedented manner for "dishes."

Six colors were introduced in 1939: Seafoam Blue, Granite Grey, Chartreuse Curry, Coral, Bean Brown, and White. Bean Brown was the first color dropped from the line during the war years, when the production of any product with uranium—in the form of red paint—was halted. Bean was replaced in 1950 or early 1951 with Black Chutney, a darker and more mottled brown glaze. Seafoam was also replaced at this time with Cedar Green and several new pieces were added to the line, including the covered pitcher, stack set, individual ramekin, divided vegetable, hostess plate, and handleless mug.

Despite its success, American Modern had its share of problems. Glaze uniformity was an incessant problem with customers and vendors complaining of the inability to match pieces. Similarly, the porous nature of the clay and the instability of the glazes caused an excessive amount of crazing—the process by which small cracks in the glaze become visible and allow for the absorption of liquid. Certain colors, like Chartreuse, Seafoam, and White were especially prone to crazing, even before the dinnerware was used. This was an issue of great concern to Russel Wright and the subject of much correspondence between him and the chemists at Steubenville.

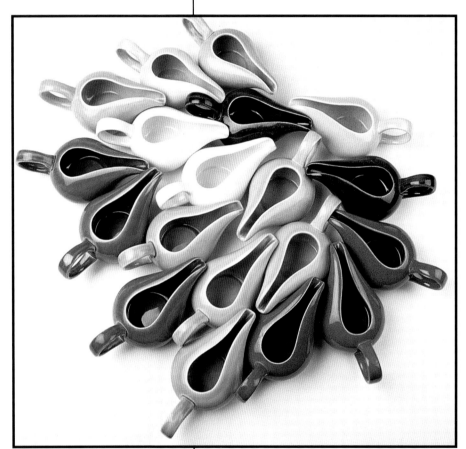

A school of creamers!

Near the end of the run, in 1955 or 1956, Cantaloupe and Glacier were added to the line. While most department stores did not carry these colors, enough was produced to make it collectible today. However, not all pieces were made in these colors.

The origins of "Steubenville Blue" are a mystery. Some have hypothesized that it was simply a glazing error. This seems unlikely, however, due to the number and variety of pieces that have surfaced. It was probably a test color or special order that had a very limited run. A couple of small sets and a few serving pieces have turned up, as well as a couple of pieces of Steubenville's Woodfield line, in this medium blue glaze.

Steubenville, like many of the Ohio River potteries, had financial difficulties for most of the post-depression era. In the late

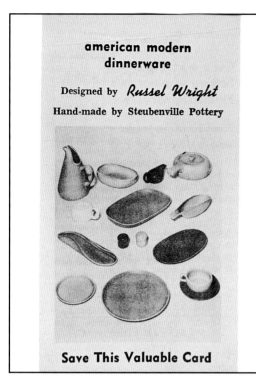

american modern
dinnerware

Designed by *Russel Wright*

Hand-made by Steubenville Pottery

Save This Valuable Card

Save

Get a 4-pc. Place Setting of America's Finest Dinnerware

for $10.00 in trade and $1.59

With every card punched out you get a 4-pc. place setting for only $1.59 Standard retail value is $3.45 you save $1.86.

Also with card—
A Creamer & sugar, $4.25
B Platter, veg. dish, $5.25
C Salt & pepper; gravy & pickle, $5.45
D Pitcher, celery, casserole, $10.20

POWERS DRUG CO.
Temple, Texas

American Modern discount ordering card.

1930s, the company's financial difficulties allowed Russel Wright greater control in every aspect of production and distribution. His dinnerware's success was the lifeblood of this company for nearly twenty years. More than 70 million pieces of American Modern were made with gross sales of over $150 million. Despite the success of this line, the company's financial difficulties forced it to close in 1959.

There has been some interest in reviving this line. In the mid-1970s, the Homer Laughlin Co. was approached to recreate American Modern. Prototypes were created in a color closely resembling the old Coral. Bloomingdale's, however, felt it would be a line with limited appeal. Instead, Homer Laughlin's Fiestaware line was reintroduced with incredible success. At the time of publication of this book, rumors persist about a current attempt to reintroduce Russel Wright's American Modern dinnerware.

Seafoam salad bowl.

American Modern pitchers and salad bowls.

Coral and Granite Grey

Coral and Granite Grey dinnerware was created in greater numbers than any of the other colors. They are the most frequently seen colors in today's secondary market. The popularity of Coral has lessened in recent years, although it is still collected. Grey is currently in great demand, but fortunately there is a large supply of it as well. All pieces were produced in these colors.

While all Russel Wright dinnerware is prone to glaze variances, Coral American Modern is found with wide and somewhat incompatible differences. The pale, washed-out Coral does not mix well with other Russel Wright glazes. The heavier, darker Coral is in much greater demand than the pale. Differences will also be found in the amount of speckling in the glaze, although most collectors are not as concerned about this difference.

There is a short supply and great demand for grey salad plates. All American

Coral carafe $200-225, Grey pitcher $85-95, Coral ice box jar $200-250, Grey covered butter $250-275.

Modern salad plates are more difficult to find than dinner plates, because of the marketing of sets without salad plates, but for some reason, grey salads are especially difficult to find.

Clockwise from center: Coral chop plate $35-40, Grey relish rosette $250-275, Coral demitasse coffeepot $75-85, Grey handled divided relish $250-275, Coral teapot $85-95, Grey coffeepot $200-225.

Coral 10" dinner plate $8-10, Grey 8" salad plate $15-18, Coral 6" bread and butter plate $3-4, Coral lug soup $12-15, Grey lug fruit $10-12.

Original Russel Wright pamphlet.

Grey hostess plate $75-85, Coral salad bowl $65-75, Grey covered ramekin $225-250, Coral celery $20-25, Grey salad fork and spoon $60-65 each.

Grey child's plate (looks like a bowl) $100-125, Coral child's bowl (this piece doubles as the base to the ramekin) $85-95, Grey child's tumbler $100-125, Coral demitasse cup/saucer $20-25.

Grey hostess plate $75-85, Coral cup $5-7.

Grey pickle dish (gravy boat underliner) with label from the Andy Warhol collection. With label $75-100, without label $18-20.

Grey baker—one of the most functional bowls in the line, but fairly scarce $40-45, Coral sauceboat $45-50.

Steubenville backstamp on most American Modern pieces.

Steubenville backstamp on advertising coaster.

Grey vegetable bowl $20-25, Coral tumbler $75-100, Grey coaster 20-22, Coral advertising coaster "Ohio State Automobile Association 1902-1952" $50-60.

Coral platter $20-25, Grey platter $25-30.

Coral stick-handled casserole $25-30, Grey covered vegetable $40-45, Coral salt and pepper $12-15 set, Grey coffee cup cover $125-150, Grey cup and saucer $10-12.

American Modern box for sugar and creamer. Box only, $25-30.

Coral pitcher, $85-95.

Coral covered pitcher $250-275, Coral stack set (lids are frequently damaged) with perfect lid $250-275, Grey covered ramekin $225-250, Grey divided vegetable $75-85.

Grey sugar $15-20, Coral creamer $12-15, Coral gravy $20-25, Grey pickle $18-20.

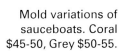

Mold variations of sauceboats. Coral $45-50, Grey $50-55.

204 intriguing ground meat recipes 108

THE *Ground Meat* COOKBOOK

The Ground Meat Cookbook. American Modern pictured throughout; very common. $10-12

Steubenville flatsoups dipped in American Modern glazes, coral and grey, $15-20 each. We have no reason to believe these are Russel Wright designs.

Coral

Item	Price
Bowl, baker	$30-35
Bowl, lug fruit	$10-12
Bowl, lug soup	$12-15
Bowl, salad	$65-75
Bowl, sauceboat	$45-50
Bowl, vegetable	$20-25
Butter dish, covered	$250-275
Carafe	$200-225
Casserole, stick handled	$25-30
Celery	$20-25
Coaster	$15-18
Coffee cup cover	$100-125
Coffeepot, 8"	$200-225
Coffeepot demitasse	$75-85
Child's bowl	$85-95
Child's plate	$75-85
Child's tumbler	$100-125
Creamer	$12-15
Cup	$5-7
Cup, demitasse	$18-20
Gravy	$20-25
Ice Box Jar	$200-250
Mug/tumbler	$75-100
Pickle	$15-18
Pitcher, tall water	$85-95
Pitcher, covered	$250-275
Plate, 6" Bread and Butter	$3-4
Plate, 8" Salad	$10-12
Plate 10" Dinner	$8-10
Plate chop	$35-40
Plate, hostess	$60-65
Platter	$20-25
Ramekin	$175-200
Relish, divided reed handle	$250-275
Relish rosette	$200-225
Salad Fork	$50-60
Salad Spoon	$50-60
Saucer	$1-2
Saucer, demitasse	$6-8
Shaker, s&p set	$12-15
Stack Server	$250-275
Sugar	$18-20
Teapot	$85-95
Vegetable, covered	$40-45
Vegetable, divided	$75-85

Granite Grey

Bowl, baker	$40-45
Bowl, lug fruit	$10-12
Bowl, lug soup	$12-15
Bowl, salad	$75-85
Bowl, sauceboat	$50-55
Bowl, vegetable	$20-25
Butter dish, covered	$250-275
Carafe	$225-250
Casserole, stick handled	$25-30
Celery	$25-30
Coaster	$20-22
Coffee cup cover	$125-150
Coffeepot, 8"	$200-225
Coffeepot demitasse	$75-85
Child's bowl	$85-95
Child's plate	$100-125
Child's tumbler	$100-125
Creamer	$15-18
Cup	$8-10
Cup, demitasse	$18-20
Gravy	$20-25
Ice Box Jar	$200-225
Mug/tumbler	$75-100
Pickle	$18-20
Pitcher, tall water	$85-95
Pitcher, covered	$300-325
Plate, 6" Bread and Butter	$3-5
Plate, 8" Salad	$15-18
Plate, 10" Dinner	$10-12
Plate chop	$35-40
Plate, hostess	$75-85
Platter	$25-30
Ramekin	$225-250
Relish, divided reed handle	$250-275
Relish rosette	$250-275
Salad Fork	$60-65
Salad Spoon	$60-65
Saucer	$1-2
Saucer, demitasse	$5-7
Shaker, s&p set	$15-18
Stack Server	$275-300
Sugar	$15-20
Teapot	$100-125
Vegetable, covered	$40-45
Vegetable, divided	$75-85

Seafoam and Chartreuse

Seafoam and Chartreuse American Modern wonderfully compliment each other and create an impressive dinner service. Both are original colors to the line, yet Seafoam was discontinued in the early 1950s. Chartreuse has recently regained its popularity; whereas Seafoam simply continues to be the most sought after of the original colors in this line.

Both Seafoam and Chartreuse are prone to crazing. With Seafoam, the crazing tends to be very small and uniform over an entire piece. This micro-crazing does not seem to detract from the overall appearance of the pottery or its collectibility. With Chartreuse, however, the crazing frequently is found in long lines that look like cracks. This crazing frequently absorbs dirt and greatly diminishes both the appearance and value of the pottery.

A variety of Seafoam glazes are found. They mix well with the other colors, but not with each other. Some distinguish the two most prevalent differences simply as "Seafoam Green" and "Seafoam Blue".

Seafoam chop plate $40-50, Chartreuse stack set $250-275, Chartreuse covered pitcher $300-325, Seafoam ice box jar $250-275.

Seafoam teapot $100-125, Chartreuse hostess plate $80-90, Seafoam pitcher $100-125, Chartreuse covered butter $275-300, Seafoam salt and pepper set $20-25.

Chartreuse coffeepot $225-250, Seafoam relish rosette $225-250, Chartreuse carafe $225-250, Seafoam salad bowl $100-125.

Seafoam carafe with wood and cork stopper. With stopper, $800-1000. Carafe only, $250-275.

Seafoam lug soup $12-15, Chartreuse cup and saucer $10-12, Seafoam 6" bread and butter plate $5-7, Chartreuse 8" salad plate $12-15, Seafoam 10" dinner plate $18-20, Chartreuse lug soup $10-12.

Chartreuse stick-handled casserole $40-45, Seafoam platter $40-45, Chartreuse demitasse coffeepot $75-85, Seafoam celery $40-45, Chartreuse salt and pepper set $18-20.

Seafoam tumbler $100-125, Seafoam coaster $20-22, Chartreuse vegetable bowl $25-30, Seafoam covered vegetable $65-75, Chartreuse coaster $18-20, Seafoam demitasse cup and saucer $20-25, Chartreuse child's tumbler $90-100.

Advertisement from *Better Homes and Gardens*, February 1950.

Chartreuse covered ramekin $200-225, Seafoam divided relish $300-325, Chartreuse covered pitcher $300-325.

Chartreuse gravy $30-35, Seafoam pickle $20-25, Chartreuse fork $65-75, Seafoam spoon $85-95.

Seafoam refrigerator jar $250-275, Chartreuse divided vegetable $100-125, Chartreuse creamer $15-18, Chartreuse sugar $20-25, Seafoam pickle $20-25.

Chartreuse sugar and creamer with original box.

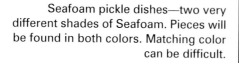

Seafoam pickle dishes—two very different shades of Seafoam. Pieces will be found in both colors. Matching color can be difficult.

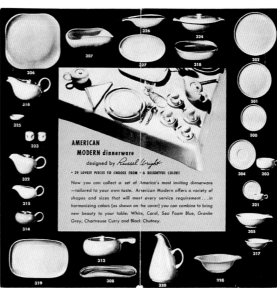

American Modern
brochure. $40-50

Chartreuse platter $30-35, Chartreuse ice box $225-250, Seafoam ice box jar $250-275.

Seafoam demitasse cup and saucer with label "Banquet, Employer-Employee, May 13, 1953." $50-75

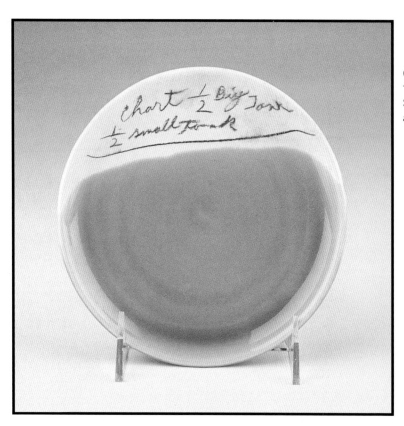

Chartreuse 6" test plate. States "Chart 1/2 Big Tank, 1/2 small tank." Shows how glaze was mixed to get a specific color. Rare, $40-50.

Chartreuse decorated coaster/ashtray with racist scene. This is probably an after-factory piece that was decorated by one of the many decorating companies in the Ohio/West Virginia area. $40-50

Seafoam Blue

Bowl, baker	$50-60
Bowl, lug fruit	$12-15
Bowl, lug soup	$12-15
Bowl, salad	$100-125
Bowl, sauceboat	$65-75
Bowl, vegetable	$30-35
Butter dish, covered	???
Carafe	$250-275
Casserole, stick handled	$40-45
Celery	$40-45
Coaster	$20-22
Coffee cup cover	???
Coffeepot, 8"	$250-275
Coffeepot demitasse	$100-125
Child's bowl	???
Child's plate	???
Child's tumbler	???
Creamer	$15-18
Cup	$10-12
Cup, demitasse	$12-15
Gravy	$30-35
Ice Box Jar	$250-275
Mug/tumbler	$100-125
Pickle	$20-25
Pitcher, tall water	$100-125
Pitcher, covered	???
Plate, 6" Bread and Butter	$5-7
Plate, 8" Salad	$20-22
Plate, 10" Dinner	$18-20
Plate chop	$40-50
Plate, hostess	???
Platter	$40-45
Ramekin	???
Relish, divided reed handle	$300-325
Relish rosette	$225-250
Salad Fork	$85-95
Salad Spoon	$85-95
Saucer	$2-3
Saucer, demitasse	$8-10
Shaker, s&p set	$20-25
Stack Server	???
Sugar	$20-25
Teapot	$100-125
Vegetable, covered	$65-75
Vegetable, divided	$125-150

Chartreuse Curry

Bowl, baker	$40-45
Bowl, lug fruit	$10-12
Bowl, lug soup	$10-12
Bowl, salad	$75-85
Bowl, sauceboat	$45-50
Bowl, vegetable	$25-30
Butter dish, covered	$275-300
Carafe	$225-250
Casserole, stick handled	$40-45
Celery	$25-30
Coaster	$18-20
Coffee cup cover	$100-125
Coffeepot, 8"	$225-250
Coffeepot demitasse	$75-85
Child's bowl	$75-100
Child's plate	$75-85
Child's tumbler	$90-100
Creamer	$15-18
Cup	$8-10
Cup, demitasse	$18-20
Gravy	$20-25
Ice Box Jar	$225-250
Mug/tumbler	$75-90
Pickle	$18-20
Pitcher, tall water	$85-95
Pitcher, covered	$300-325
Plate, 6" Bread and Butter	$4-5
Plate, 8" Salad	$12-15
Plate, 10" Dinner	$10-12
Plate chop	$35-40
Plate, hostess	$80-90
Platter	$30-35
Ramekin	$200-225
Relish, divided reed handle	$250-275
Relish rosette	$200-225
Salad Fork	$65-75
Salad Spoon	$65-75
Saucer	$1-2
Saucer, demitasse	$8-10
Shaker, s&p set	$18-20
Stack Server	$250-275
Sugar	$20-25
Teapot	$95-105
Vegetable, covered	$35-45
Vegetable, divided	$100-125

Cedar Green and Black Chutney

Cedar Green and Black Chutney were not original colors. Exactly when they came into the line is difficult to determine. Black Chutney was introduced in the early 1950s, to replace Bean Brown, which had been dropped during the war years because of its red color content. Cedar also makes its appearance in company literature in the early 1950s when Seafoam was dropped from the line. There does not seem to be a time when Seafoam and Cedar were both available.

Black Chutney is an extremely dark color and is frequently found with wonderful mottling. Like many of Russel Wright's glazes for other lines, each piece of Black Chutney is different. Today, Cedar is one of the most sought after of American Modern colors. Unfortunately, not a great deal of the flatware is found. Many of the later pieces to the line are found more frequently in Cedar than in other colors, especially the stack set.

Cedar pitcher $175-185, Black Chutney pitcher $125-135, Black Chutney salad bowl $75-85, Cedar vegetable $40-45.

All Cedar pieces. Covered butter dish $350-400, vegetable bowl $40-45, divided vegetable $150-175, salad bowl $125-150, tumbler $125-150, gravy $40-45.

Cedar stack set $325-350, Black Chutney stack set $275-300.

American Modern pamphlet.

Cedar chop plate $50-60, Black Chutney stack set $275-300, Cedar tumbler $125-150, Cedar demitasse cup and saucer $40-50, Black Chutney gravy $25-30, Black Chutney coffee-pot $225-250.

All Black Chutney. Demitasse coffeepot $100-125, vegetable bowl $25-30, baker $50-55, covered vegetable $50-60, celery $25-30, covered ramekin $225-250.

Black Chutney cup and saucer $10-12, Cedar dinner $20-22, Black Chutney 8" salad plate $18-20, Cedar 6" bread and butter plate $5-7, Cedar lug fruit $12-15, Black Chutney lug soup $12-15.

American Modern ordering pamphlets. $20-25 each

Cedar coffeepot (The coffeepot is most frequently seen in this color) $225-250, Cedar demitasse coffeepot $125-150, Black Chutney platter $25-30, Black Chutney salt and pepper $20-25 set, Black Chutney sauceboat $50-55.

Cedar hostess plate $100-125, Black Chutney tumbler $90-100, Cedar tumbler $125-150, Black Chutney covered butter $300-350.

Cedar creamer, $20-25.

Cedar child's plate $100-125, Cedar child's tumbler $150-175, Black Chutney child's bowl $100-125.

Cedar teapot (scarce) $225-250, Cedar demitasse coffeepot $125-150, Black Chutney stick-handled casserole $45-50, Cedar shaker $12-15 each, Black Chutney shaker $10-12 each.

Black Chutney divided vegetable $100-125, Cedar gravy $40-45, Black Chutney pickle $20-25, Cedar cup and saucer $12-15, Black Chutney coffee cup cover $100-125.

Two mold variations of American Modern covered butter dishes.

Cedar Green

Bowl, baker	$50-60
Bowl, lug fruit	$12-15
Bowl, lug soup	$16-18
Bowl, salad	$125-150
Bowl, sauceboat	$65-75
Bowl, vegetable	$40-45
Butter dish, covered	???
Carafe	$300-350
Casserole, stick handled	$90-100
Celery	$40-45
Coaster	$35-40
Coffee cup cover	$150-175
Coffeepot, 8"	$225-250
Coffeepot demitasse	$125-150
Child's bowl	$100-125
Child's plate	$100-125
Child's tumbler	$150-175
Creamer	$20-25
Cup	$10-12
Cup, demitasse	$30-35
Gravy	$40-45
Ice Box Jar	???
Mug/tumbler	$125-150
Pickle	$35-40
Pitcher, tall water	$175-185
Pitcher, covered	$375-400
Plate, 6" Bread and Butter	$5-7
Plate, 8" Salad	$20-25
Plate, 10" Dinner	$20-22
Plate chop	$50-60
Plate, hostess	$100-125
Platter	$40-50
Ramekin	$300-325
Relish, divided reed handle	$350-400
Relish rosette	????
Salad Fork	????
Salad Spoon	????
Saucer	$3-5
Saucer, demitasse	$10-12
Shaker, s&p set	$25-30
Stack Server	$325-350
Sugar	$20-25
Teapot	$225-250
Vegetable, covered	$75-85
Vegetable, divided	$150-175

Black Chutney

Item	Price
Bowl, baker	$50-55
Bowl, lug fruit	$12-15
Bowl, lug soup	$12-15
Bowl, salad	$75-85
Bowl, sauceboat	$50-55
Bowl, vegetable	$25-30
Butter dish, covered	$300-350
Carafe	???
Casserole, stick handled	$45-50
Celery	$25-30
Coaster	$15-18
Coffee cup cover	$100-125
Coffeepot, 8"	$225-250
Coffeepot demitasse	$100-125
Child's bowl	$100-125
Child's plate	$75-100
Child's tumbler	$100-125
Creamer	$15-18
Cup	$8-10
Cup, demitasse	$18-20
Gravy	$25-30
Ice Box Jar	???
Mug/tumbler	$90-100
Pickle	$20-25
Pitcher, tall water	$125-135
Pitcher, covered	$300-350
Plate, 6" Bread and Butter	$4-6
Plate, 8" Salad	$18-20
Plate 10" Dinner	$15-18
Plate chop	$35-40
Plate, hostess	$60-65
Platter	$25-30
Ramekin	$225-250
Relish, divided reed handle	???
Relish rosette	???
Salad Fork	???
Salad Spoon	???
Saucer	$2-4
Saucer, demitasse	$8-10
Shaker, s&p set	$20-25
Stack Server	$275-300
Sugar	$18-20
Teapot	$100-125
Vegetable, covered	$50-60
Vegetable, divided	$100-125

White and Glacier Blue

White and Glacier American Modern pieces are highly sought after. Despite the fact that White was produced for the entire run, very little of it in good condition has survived. White dinnerware crazes very badly and this crazing tends to darken and stain with use. Decorated White dinnerware is found with both Russel Wright-approved geometric designs and with a variety of decals that were not approved by Russel Wright.

Glacier, like Cantaloupe, was only produced for a few years at the end of the run (1955-1959), when the company was having extreme financial difficulties. It was not heavily distributed and most of the major department stores never added it to their line. Unlike Cantaloupe, Glacier dinner plates are very difficult to find. No carafes have been reported in Glacier. Glacier is one of the glazes that is frequently found with very light pre-crazing. If you look at a piece from different angles you can almost always catch this glaze imperfection. Glacier dinnerware also tends to craze when it gets wet. A seemingly perfect piece will often turn out to be horribly crazed after being submerged in water. Sometimes this crazing dries out.

Glacier pitcher $500-600, White chop plate $100-125, Glacier salt and pepper $25-30 set, White butter $500-600.

White demitasse cup and saucer $45-50, Glacier demitasse coffeepot $150-175, White coffeepot $300-350.

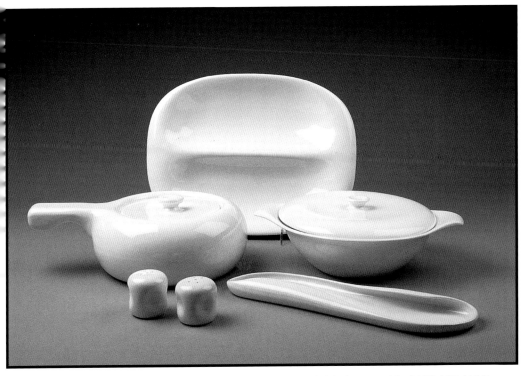

White stick-handled casserole $100-125, White divided vegetable $150-175, White covered vegetable $100-125, White celery $40-50, White salt and pepper $25-30/set.

White lug fruit $20-25, Glacier 6" bread and butter plate $10-12, White tumbler $150-175, White coffee cup cover $150-175, Glacier cup $12-15, White saucer $3-5, White 10" dinner $20-25, Glacier 8" salad plate $40-45, White 6" bread and butter plate $8-10, Glacier lug soup $25-30.

White hostess plate $125-150, Glacier cup $12-15, White dinner $20-25, Glacier 6" bread and butter $10-12, White child's tumbler $200-225.

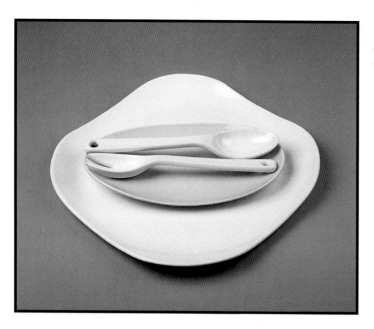

White chop plate $100-125, Glacier pickle $50-60, White fork and spoon $200-250/set.

Glacier coffeepot, $500-600.

White. Covered ramekin $300-325, salad bowl $125-150, stack set $325-350.

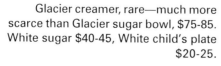

Glacier creamer, rare—much more scarce than Glacier sugar bowl, $75-85. White sugar $40-45, White child's plate $20-25.

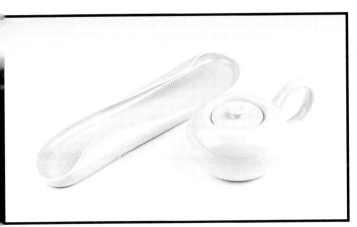

Glacier celery $75-85, sugar $40-45

White platter $65-75, Glacier pickle $50-60, White gravy $50-60.

White. Pitcher $200-225, teapot $175-200, cup and saucer $18-20, coffee cup cover $150-175.

White. Salad bowl $125-150, small baker $40-50, sauceboat $65-75, lug fruit $20-25, vegetable bowl $50-60.

White carafe, $325-350.

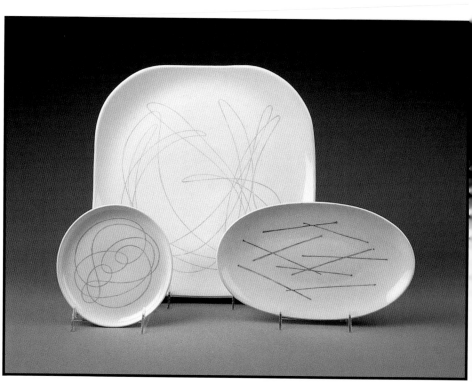

Spencerian 6" plate $20-25, Spencerian chop
plate $125-150, Match Sticks pickle $45-50.

White relish rosette, $450-500.

Pitcher with floral decal $125-150, lug soup with floral decal $15-20.

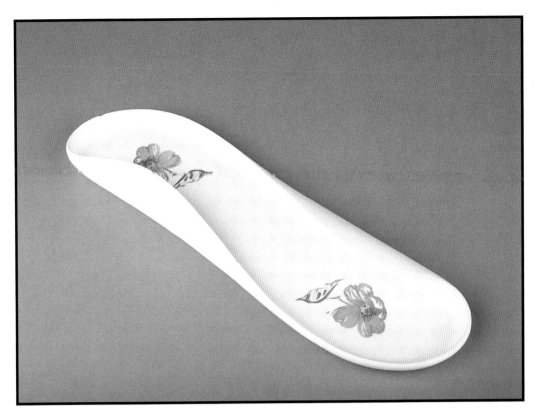

Celery with floral decal, $40-45.

Chutney Leaf dinnerware. Scarce.

White

Item	Price
Bowl, baker	40-50
Bowl, lug fruit	$20-25
Bowl, lug soup	$25-30
Bowl, salad	$125-150
Bowl, sauceboat	$65-75
Bowl, vegetable	$50-60
Butter dish, covered	$500-600
Carafe	$325-350
Casserole, stick handled	$100-125
Celery	$40-50
Coaster	$25-30
Coffee cup cover	$150-175
Coffeepot, 8"	$300-350
Coffeepot demitasse	$200-225
Child's bowl	$175-200
Child's plate	$150-175
Child's tumbler	$200-225
Creamer	$50-60
Cup	$16-18
Cup, demitasse	$45-40
Gravy	$50-60
Ice Box Jar	$375-400
Mug/tumbler	$150-175
Pickle	$35-40
Pitcher, tall water	$200-225
Pitcher, covered	$400-450
Plate, 6" Bread and Butter	$8-10
Plate, 8" Salad	$20-25
Plate, 10" Dinner	$20-25
Plate chop	$100-125
Plate, hostess	$125-150
Platter	$65-75
Ramekin	$300-325
Relish divided reed handle	$350-375
Relish rosette	$450-500
Salad Fork	$100-125
Salad Spoon	$100-125
Saucer	$3-5
Saucer, demitasse	$10-12
Shaker, s&p set	$25-30
Stack Server	$325-350
Sugar	$40-45
Teapot	$175-200
Vegetable, covered	$100-125
Vegetable, divided	$150-175

Glacier Blue

Bowl, baker	$75-85
Bowl, lug fruit	$20-22
Bowl, lug soup	$25-30
Bowl, salad	$300-350
Bowl, sauceboat	$100-125
Bowl, vegetable	$60-70
Butter dish, covered	$800-1000
Carafe	???
Casserole, stick handled	$125-150
Celery	$75-85
Coaster	$25-30
Coffee cup cover	???
Coffeepot, 8"	$500-600
Coffeepot demitasse	$150-175
Child's bowl	$200-225
Child's plate	$200-225
Child's tumbler	???
Creamer	$75-85
Cup	$12-15
Cup, demitasse	???
Gravy	$65-75
Ice Box Jar	???
Mug/tumbler	???
Pickle	$50-60
Pitcher, tall water	$500-600
Pitcher, covered	$750-850
Plate, 6" Bread and Butter	$10-12
Plate, 8" Salad	$40-45
Plate, 10" Dinner	$45-50
Plate chop	$100-125
Plate, hostess	$250-275
Platter	$100-125
Ramekin	???
Relish, divided reed handle	???
Relish rosette	???
Salad Fork	$125-150
Salad Spoon	$125-150
Saucer	$8-10
Saucer, demitasse	$25-30
Shaker, s&p set	$25-30
Stack Server	$800-1000
Sugar	$40-45
Teapot	$375-450
Vegetable, covered	$90-100
Vegetable, divided	$225-250

Bean Brown and Cantaloupe

Although Cantaloupe and Bean Brown look great together, the difference in their production dates makes it unlikely that they were used together. Like other "red" glazed American dinnerware, Bean Brown was discontinued during the war. This helps to explain its relative rarity today.

Many of the pieces that were added in the early 1950s should not be found in Bean Brown, including the covered pitcher, stack set, ramekin, coffee cup cover, hostess plate, and child's pieces.

Cantaloupe was added extremely late to the line in the mid-1950s. Most pieces are extremely scarce today. This color is often confused with Coral; Cantaloupe is orange, not pink.

Many pieces have not been reported in Cantaloupe. We have only priced items that we have seen or for which we have received reliable reports. We have not heard of many of the more impressive pieces in the line existing in Cantaloupe including butter dish, covered pitcher, relish rosette, and demitasse pieces. These pieces may exist. Please let us know if you have seen them.

Cantaloupe pitcher $500-550, Bean Brown pitcher $275-300, Bean Brown demitasse coffeepot $200-225, Cantaloupe teapot $350-400, Cantaloupe salt and pepper shakers $25-30 set, Bean Brown demitasse cup and saucer $40-45.

Bean Brown relish rosette $325-350, Cantaloupe baker $100-125, Bean Brown celery $50-55.

All Bean Brown. Salad bowl $150-175, chop plate $85-100, platter $65-75, vegetable bowl $45-50, salt and pepper $25-35, teapot $200-225.

Bean brown cup and saucer $18-20, Cantaloupe 6" bread and butter plate $10-12, Bean Brown 8" salad plate $30-35, Cantaloupe 10" dinner $18-20.

Two different shades of Bean Brown. $25-35 set.

Cantaloupe pitcher $500-550, Bean brown divided relish $325-350.

American Modern advertisement from *House Beautiful*, May 1951.

Cantaloupe sugar $45-50, creamer $40-45, celery $100-125, covered casserole $125-150, cup/saucer $18-20.

Two Bean Brown carafes. Notice that the design for the carafe with stopper has an opening with a lip to hold the stopper in place. Carafe $300-325, Carafe with original wood and cork stopper $750-1000. The stopper for this item is wood and cork, not simply wood. Several have recently been made of solid wood!

Bean Brown

Bowl, baker	$75-100
Bowl, lug fruit	$18-20
Bowl, lug soup	$18-20
Bowl, salad	$150-175
Bowl, sauceboat	$75-100
Bowl, vegetable	$45-50
Butter dish, covered	???
Carafe	$300-325
Casserole, stick handled	$65-75
Celery	$50-55
Coaster	$40-45
Coffee cup cover	n/a
Coffeepot, 8"	???
Coffeepot demitasse	$200-225
Child's bowl	n/a
Child's plate	n/a
Child's tumbler	n/a
Creamer	$25-30
Cup	$15-18
Cup, demitasse	$30-35
Gravy	$50-60
Ice Box Jar	$250-275
Mug/tumbler	n/a
Pickle	$35-45
Pitcher, tall water	$275-300
Pitcher, covered	n/a
Plate, 6" Bread and Butter	$10-12
Plate, 8" Salad	$30-35
Plate, 10" Dinner	$20-25
Plate, chop	$85-100
Plate, hostess	n/a
Platter	$65-75
Ramekin	n/a
Relish, divided reed handle	$325-350
Relish rosette	$325-350
Salad Fork	???
Salad Spoon	???
Saucer	$3-5
Saucer, demitasse	$10-12
Shaker, s&p set	$25-35
Stack Server	n/a
Sugar	$30-35
Teapot	$200-225
Vegetable, covered	$100-125
Vegetable, divided	n/a

Cantaloupe

Bowl, baker	$100-125
Bowl, lug fruit	$35-40
Bowl, lug soup	$40-45
Bowl, salad	???
Bowl, sauceboat	$100-125
Bowl, vegetable	$100-125
Butter dish, covered	???
Carafe	???
Casserole, stick handled	$125-150
Celery	$100-125
Coaster	???
Coffee cup cover	???
Coffeepot, 8"	???
Coffeepot demitasse	???
Child's bowl	???
Child's plate	???
Child's tumbler	???
Creamer	$40-45
Cup	$12-15
Cup, demitasse	???
Gravy	$75-100
Ice Box Jar	???
Mug/tumbler	???
Pickle	$50-55
Pitcher, tall water	$500-550
Pitcher, covered	???
Plate, 6" Bread and Butter	$10-12
Plate, 8" Salad	$40-45
Plate, 10" Dinner	$18-20
Plate chop	$125-150
Plate, hostess	???
Platter	$125-150
Ramekin	???
Relish, divided reed handle	???
Relish rosette	???
Salad Fork	???
Salad Spoon	???
Saucer	$6-8
Saucer, demitasse	???
Shaker, s&p set	$25-30
Stack Server	???
Sugar	$45-50
Teapot	$350-400
Vegetable, covered	$125-150
Vegetable, divided	???

Steubenville Blue

Although many collectors have their theories about the origins of Steubenville blue, no documentation exists of this color. Only a handful of pieces have been reported: three sizes of plates, demitasse and regular cups and saucers, lug soup, covered vegetable, salt and pepper, and chop plate. Surely, other pieces exist. A few pieces of Steubenville's Woodfield line have also been found in this glaze.

Steubenville Blue casserole (center). Steubenville Blue demitasse cup, $200-250. Shown with Chartreuse and Seafoam.

Steubenville Blue covered casserole. Extremely rare, $1000-1250.

Steubenville Blue 6" bread and butter plate $100-125, dinner plate $250-275, cup and saucer $200-250, demitasse cup and saucer $300-350.

Additional American Modern Pieces and Prototypes

Ideal plastic children's set. Complete service for four, $90-100. Cup and saucer $3-4, plates $4-5, sugar and creamer set $10-15, demitasse pot $15-20, gravy boat $10-15, silverware $1-2 each, covered vegetable $15-18, platter $8-10.

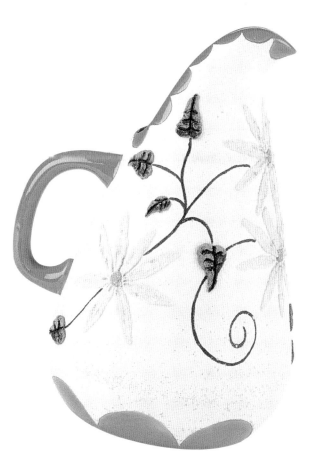

Crude pitcher of unknown origin. Handle is applied upside down. We have seen a similar pitcher done in red, white, and blue. Equally as attractive! $100-150.

Grey creamer in an experimental glaze with trial numbers on bottom. Scarce $75-100.

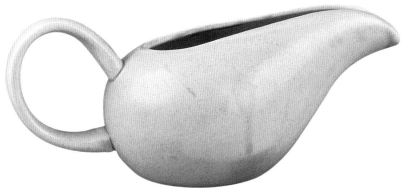

Lug soup with metallic glaze and Russel Wright backstamp. $100-150

Unglazed stick-handled casserole. How did this piece survive? $75-100

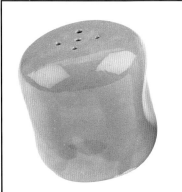

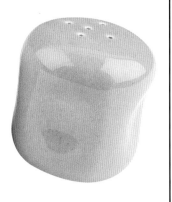

Pink salt shaker. Not Steubenville. Shown next to Cantaloupe shaker. Unknown origin.

Dark green platter, shown with Seafoam and Cedar creamers for comparison. Trial glaze color—extremely rare. $150-175

Comparison of old American Modern cup above and Homer Laughlin cup below.

American Modern re-issue by Homer Laughlin. Trial pieces for line proposed to Bloomingdale's. This line never went into production. Color is between Coral and Cantaloupe. All pieces extremely rare. We do not know of any pieces making it into the marketplace. NV

Two-handled Homer Laughlin bowl, one-handled original lug soup.

Homer Laughlin bowl on top of American Modern plate.

Iroquois Casual China

Russel Wright advertising plate. Advertising that the dinnerware is "replaced if it breaks." $250-275

While American Modern was an experiment riddled with unsolvable problems, Iroquois Casual was a work-in-progress that demonstrated Russel Wright's active role in the life of the dinnerware line. Created in 1947, the line went through three distinct periods, with colors and pieces being added and dropped from the line, before it was discontinued in 1966.

The dinnerware line was quite simple during the first period, 1947-1949. It was a group of multipurpose pieces done in a heavy clay and available in four foamy/mottled colors: Oyster White, Powder Blue, Brown, and Chartreuse Yellow. Like the art pottery of the period, the glaze on each piece varied, having a raindrop effect in the center of the piece.

The line was greatly expanded in 1949 with the addition of colors and pieces. The early glazes were abandoned for smooth even colors and the thickness of the china was greatly reduced. For these reasons, the early dinnerware and that of the post-1949 period do not mix well. The colors added to the line in 1949 were

Iroquois stacking sugars and creamers.

Iroquois carafes and redesigned pitchers.

Oyster Grey, Parsley Green, Avocado Yellow, Sugar White, Nutmeg Brown, and Ice Blue. Ripe Apricot was added in 1950.

With the change in color and thickness, came a change in the marketing of the line. Russel Wright took a primary role in the distribution and advertising of the product. Central to the advertising campaign was the durability of the product. To emphasize this fact, the line was briefly renamed "Duralaine Casual China." In addition to being durable, the ads stressed the multiple uses of the pieces. "Serve in it! Store in it! Bake in it!," was the lead on one advertising pamphlet. Similarly one ad read that the teapot also doubled as the pitcher when its cover was taken off.

Oyster and Parsley stayed in production for only about six years. Both were dropped from company literature by 1956. These colors are extremely popular today and are relatively scarce. No redesigned pieces should be found in these colors.

During the mid-1950s, Russel Wright worked with Iroquois on redesigning or re-styling the line. The archives in Syracuse are filled with his attempts to alter pieces to make them more visually appealing and more functional. Three different approaches were used.

First, Russel Wright redesigned the existing dinnerware, adding a small foot to virtually all pieces and changing the pinch lids of the early period to knob lids. These changes addressed the repeated complaint about the pinched lid being difficult to use,

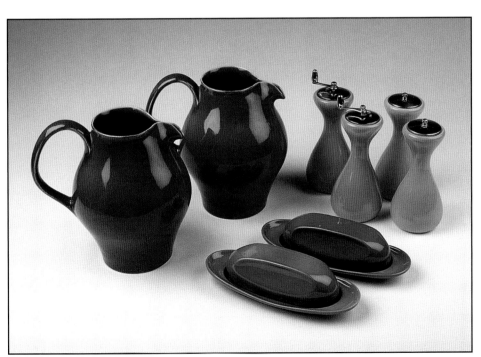

If you have to have duplicates...

while also giving the dinnerware a new look. Additional pieces were added, including the extremely popular redesigned pitcher and the beautiful, but difficult to use, redesigned gravy. The gravy is one of today's most favorite pieces, resembling a space ship when the lid/stand is being used as a lid. Overall, the redesigned set was extremely popular and boosted sales back to record levels.

The second approach, at Iroquois' suggestion, was for Russel Wright to add several floral decals to the line. Iroquois suggested this as a way to address the sluggish sales of the line in the mid-1950s and to compete with the popular floral lines of the day. While these designs were not a favorite of consumers in the 1950s or collectors today, Russel Wright seemed to spend a huge amount of time and energy in the creation of this line. His archives include thousands of drawings for this project along with flower clippings.

And finally, Russel Wright proposed a whole new line of Iroquois dinnerware which was to include some of the design elements of Iroquois Casual. The casserole at the end of the chapter is from this line. It was found as a part of a set believed to be prototypes that was discovered in the Syracuse, New York area. The designs for these pieces and the floral decals are present in the archives, but clearly the line never went into regular production.

Four final colors were added to the line in the 1960s: Cantaloupe, Brick Red, Aqua, and Mustard Gold. All are premium colors today, with Cantaloupe being somewhat scarce and Brick and Aqua being quite rare. While Mustard is also scarce, it does not receive the same enthusiasm from collectors, probably because it is not that dissimilar to the more frequently seen Avocado and Lemon Yellow dishes. Some Cantaloupe pieces will be found with the original design, but Aqua, Brick, and Mustard will only be found in redesigned pieces (with the exception of the stacking salt and pepper and the gumbo—which were the only pieces not redesigned.)

Also added to the line in the 1960s was a small cookware line that included a saucepan, six-quart dutch oven, frypan, and warming tray. A large stove-like electrical stand is also pictured in company literature and store advertisements, but none have been reported. Only a couple of the warming trays have emerged in Ripe Apricot, but more may be found in additional colors. The warming tray was quite expensive, advertised for as much as $24.95 in company price lists.

Casual China appeals to today's consumer both for its durability and variety of color. While the form of the American Modern line attracts collectors, Iroquois Casual China is great for everyday use.

Russel Wright Easter egg hunt.

Complete Guide to Iroquois Casual China by Russel Wright

Legend:
- R = redesigned
- B = both original and redesigned
- > = or later

RAINDROP/MOTTLED COLORS:
- Sugar White 1946–
- Ice Blue 1946–
- Nutmeg Brown 1946–
- Avocado Yellow 1946–

SOLID COLORS:

EARLY COLORS:
- Oyster Grey 1949–1955
- Parsley Green 1949–1956
- Avocado Yellow 1949–1960
- Sugar White 1949–1967
- Nutmeg Brown 1949–1964>
- Ice Blue 1949–1967

MIDDLE COLORS:
- Ripe Apricot 1950/51–1967
- Pink Sherbet 1954–1967
- Charcoal 1954–1964>
- Lettuce Green 1956–1967
- Lemon 1957–1967
- Cantaloupe 1959/60–1964>

LATE COLORS:
- Turquoise 1965–1967
- Brick Red 1965–1967
- Mustard Gold 1967–

Stock #	Year Introduced	Year Discontinued	R/B	Item
184	1946	1947>		Cream (large stacking)
185	1949	1957		Cup (large coffee)
188	1952	1957		Sugar (large stacking)
	1946	1947>		Teapot w/ Cover (large)
184	1949	1957		AD Coffee Cup
185	1949	1957		AD Coffee Saucer
188	1952	1957	R	Baking Tureen w/ Cover (8", 4 qt.)
153	1961	1967		Beverage Pitcher (2 qt.)
165	1961	1967	R	Beverage Pitcher w/ Cover (1.5 qt)
107	1946	1967	B	Bread & Butter Plate (6 7/16")
130	1949	1967		Butter Dish
131	1949	1964		Butter Dish Cover
183	1952	1961		Butter dish w/ Cover (1/4 lb)
151	1949	1961	R	Casserole w/ Cover (8", 2 qt, grooved)
114	1949	1963		Casserole w/ Cover (8", knob)
187	1957	1967		Chop Plate (round, 13 7/8")
130	1965	1967	R	Coffee Carafe
175	1957	1967		Coffee Mug (13 oz)
140	1947	1961	R	Cream
141	1961	1967	R	Cream (stacking)
102	1946	1961	R	Cup
172	1961	1963	R	Cup & Saucer (coffee cup)
182	1957	1967	R	Cup (inc handle)
110	1946	1967	B	Dinner Plate (10")
182	1957	1967		Divided-Veg Dish w/ Cover (10", grooved)
120	1947	1950	B	Divided-Veg Dish w/ Cover (10", knob)
172	1961	1963		Dutch Oven w/ Cover (6 qt)
141	1961	1967		Fruit
102	1946	1961		Fruit
106	1961	1963	R	Fry Pan w/ Cover
191	1963	1967	R	Gravy Bowl
191	1957	1963	R	Gravy Bowl w/ Stand (attached)
190-A	1949	1957	B	Gravy Cover
190	1957	1967	R	Gravy Cover-Stand
191-1	1957	1963	R	Gravy Stand (7 1/2")
190	1949	1957	B	Gravy/Soup Bowl (18oz)
123	1952	1967	B	Gumbo Dish (21 oz)
195	1965	1967		Individual Platter (oval, 10 1/4")
193	1946	1967	B	Large Platter (oval, 14 1/2")
109	1946	1961		Luncheon Plate
160	1946	1967	B	Round Vegetable (8", 36 oz)
195	1946	1967	B	Salad Bowl (10")
108	1946	1967	B	Salad/Dessert Plate (7 3/8")
394	1961	1963		Salt & Pepper Mill
194-SP	1949	1967		Salt and Pepper (stacking)
171	1961	1963		Saucepan w/ Cover
176	1957	1967	R	Saucer
192	1949	1967	B	Small Platter (oval, 12 3/4")
103-A	1946	1957	B	Soup Cover
103	1946	1957	B	Soup/Cereal (11 1/2 oz)
141	1961	1967	R	Sugar (stacking)
141	1961	1967	R	Sugar w Cover
183	1961	1967	R	Tall Coffee
181	1950	1959	R	Tea Cup
180	1950	1959	R	Tea Saucer
180	1961	1967	R	Teapot w/ Cover (48oz)
152	1957	1967	R	Teapot w/ Cover
150	1947	1957	R	Teapot w/ Cover
135	1954	1957		TV Buffet Plate
177	1961	1963		Warming Platter (electric)

Please note: Dates in this chart were derived from archival information, trade journals, brochures, and collector intelligence. Some dates are extrapolations based on this information, therefore date ranges are only best estimates and subject to change. This chart is based on the original copyrighted work of Dennis Mykytyn with modifications based on research by Michael Pratt. This version is updated as of April 2000 and is reproduced with the permission of Dennis Mykytyn and Michael Pratt.

Charcoal, Oyster, and White

Charcoal, Oyster, and White Iroquois Casual are among the most popular and versatile colors of any Russel Wright dinnerware. White was first introduced in 1947 as a foamy, mottled glaze frequently found with a raindrop effect. Each piece had a different glazing effect—some were foamy with few bubbles; others had lots of bubbles and resembled art pottery. In 1949, this color was transformed into Sugar White, a softer, much more even glaze. At this point the dinnerware was transformed into a much thinner and more homogenized line.

White was the most popular color in this line. Company documents illustrate that, in 1961, for example, almost 30% of the orders of Russel Wright Casual were for Sugar White; only 3% were for Charcoal. Oyster had an extremely short life, from 1949-1955, which explains its relative scarcity today. Several pieces of Oyster are in extremely short supply, especially carafes, mugs, gumbos, and covered pitchers.

A couple of the AD coffeepot lamps have turned up. We have had reports that they were part of displays to illustrate the translucent qualities of the dinnerware.

Charcoal salt and pepper mill set $800-1000, Charcoal chop plate $100-125, Oyster carafe (rare) $500-600, Oyster chop plate $100-125, White salt and pepper mill $750-850 set, White chop plate $100-125.

White carafe $250-275, Charcoal redesigned creamer $40-45, Charcoal redesigned sugar and cover $45-50, Oyster large platter $40-45, White medium platter $40-50.

Top left: Charcoal covered pitcher $200-225, White party plate $90-100, Charcoal party plate $100-125, White redesigned covered butter $500-600.

Top right: Charcoal redesigned fruit $20-25, Oyster fruit $12-15, White 6" bread and butter $4-6, Oyster 7" salad plate $15-18, Charcoal dinner $20-25.

Center left: Charcoal original three-piece gravy $100-125, Oyster medium platter $40-45, White eggcup $40-50. There is considerable disagreement over whether these eggcups are a Russel Wright design. They are not marked, but are clearly by Iroquois and are found in at least five of the Russel Wright glazes.

Bottom: From left: White original mug $125-150, Charcoal original mug $200-225, White redesigned mug $90-100, Charcoal redesigned mug $100-125.

From left: White cups and saucers, AD c/s $125-150, original c/s $10-12, redesigned c/s $10-12, early coffee c/s $20-22. Oyster cups and saucers, original c/s $10-12, AD c/s $200-250, early coffee c/s $18-20. Charcoal cups and saucers, redesigned c/s $12-15, original c/s $10-12, AD c/s $250-300.

Covered charcoal pitcher $200-225, White gumbo $70-80, Oyster gumbo (rare) $150-175, Charcoal butter $125-150.

White large platter $50-60, Charcoal covered cereal $30-35, Oyster covered cereal $30-35, White covered cereal $30-35. These lids also fit the deep soup bowl.

Charcoal: 10" serving bowl $65-75, 8" vegetable $50-60, 5" cereal $15-18. Oyster: 10" serving bowl $60-70, 8" vegetable $65-75, 5" cereal $15-18. White: 10" serving bowl $65-75, 8" vegetable $60-70, 5" cereal $15-18.

All White, from left: 2-qt. redesigned casserole $65-75, 6-qt. dutch oven $325-350, Original 2-qt. casserole $65-75, Original 4-qt. $150-175, restyled covered divided vegetable $65-75.

All White. Dutch oven $325-350, covered frypan $250-275, covered saucepan $250-275.

White carafe $250-275, Oyster chop plate $100-125, Charcoal dutch oven $750-850.

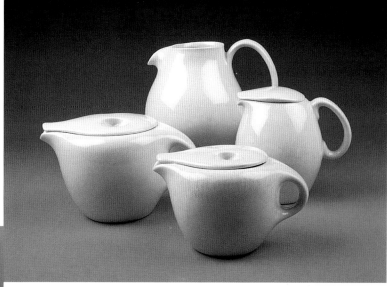

Close-up on coffeepot and AD coffeepot to illustrate foamy glazes.

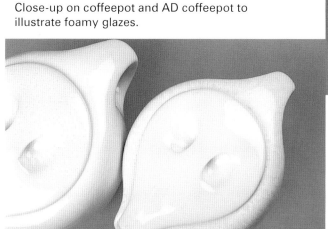

All White, from left: Coffeepot and cover (referred to in company literature as the teapot to the line, but collectors have commonly called this the coffeepot.) $150-175, redesigned pitcher $350-375, AD coffeepot (with early foamy glaze) $125-150, covered pitcher $200-225.

Oyster cereal $15-18, Charcoal deep soup $50-60, White original fruit $18-20.

White stacking sugar and creamer $40-45, Charcoal stacking sugar and creamer $45-50, Oyster stacking sugar and creamer $40-45.

Large White platter $50-60, stacking Oyster salt and pepper $40-45, Charcoal redesigned teapot $350-400.

One of the Iroquois backstamps.

White family sugar (rare—has three indents) $65-75, White family creamer $45-50, White stacking sugar (has two indents) $20-25, White stacking creamer $15-20.

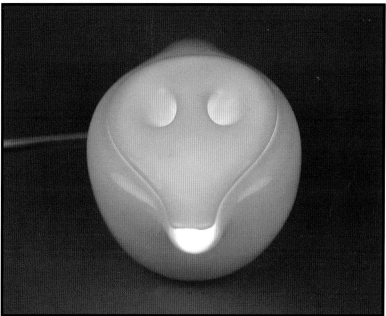

Iroquois White AD pot converted to a light. Done for promotional display. Illustrates translucence of dinnerware. We have seen a couple of these for sale in the marketplace. Rare. $250-300

Charcoal

Bowl, cereal	$15-18
Bowl, fruit original	$15-18
Bowl, fruit redesigned	$20-25
Bowl, deep soup	$50-60
Bowl, gumbo	$80-100
Bowl, 8" open vegetable	$50-60
Bowl, 10" serving bowl	$65-75
Butter dish, original	$125-150
Butter dish, redesigned	n/a
Carafe	$300-350
Casserole, 2 qt. covered	$65-75
Casserole, 4 qt. covered	$150-175
Casserole, divided covered	$65-75
Coffeepot/Teapot covered	n/a
Coffeepot AD covered	n/a
Cover for soup/cereal & gravy	$15-17
Creamer, original	$20-25
Creamer, large family	n/a
Creamer, redesigned	$40-45
Cup/Saucer original	$10-12
Cup/Saucer redesigned	$12-15
Cup/Saucer, coffee	n/a
Cup/Saucer, after dinner	$250-300
Gravy, redesigned	$500-600
Gravy, attached stand	$125-150
Mug, original	$200-225
Mug, redesigned/tall coffee	$100-125
Pitcher, 1 1/2 qt. covered	$200-225
Pitcher, redesigned	$500-600
Plate, 6" B&B	$5-7
Plate, 7" salad	$15-18
Plate, 9" lunch	$30-35
Plate, 10" dinner	$20-25
Plate, 14" chop	$125-150
Plate, party w/ cup indent	$100-125
Plate, underplate for gravy	$20-25
Platter, 10" individual	n/a
Platter, 13" oval	$40-45
Platter, 15" oval	$60-65
Salt/Pepper stacking	$40-45
Salt and Pepper Mill set	$800-1000
Sugar, original stack	$20-25
Sugar, family stack	n/a
Sugar, redesigned covered	$45-50
Teapot, redesigned	$350-400

Cookware

Dutch Oven, 6 qt., covered	$750-850
Frypan, covered	$500-600
Saucepan, covered	$500-600
Warming Tray	????

Oyster

Bowl, cereal _____ $15-18
Bowl, fruit original _____ $12-15
Bowl, fruit redesigned _____ n/a
Bowl, deep soup _____ $65-75
Bowl, gumbo _____ $150-175
Bowl, 8" open vegetable _____ $65-75
Bowl, 10" serving bowl _____ $60-70
Butter dish, original _____ $125-150
Butter dish, redesigned _____ n/a
Carafe _____ $500-600
Casserole, 2 qt. covered _____ $40-45
Casserole, 4 qt. covered _____ $125-150
Casserole, divided covered _____ $40-45
Coffeepot/Teapot covered _____ n/a
Coffeepot AD covered _____ $125-150
Cover for soup/cereal & gravy _____ $15-17
Creamer, original _____ $20-25
Creamer, large family _____ n/a
Creamer, redesigned _____ n/a
Cup/Saucer original _____ $10-12
Cup/Saucer redesigned _____ n/a
Cup/Saucer, coffee _____ $18-20
Cup/Saucer, after dinner _____ $200-250
Gravy, redesigned _____ n/a
Gravy, attached stand _____ n/a
Mug, original _____ $175-225
Mug, redesigned/tall coffee _____ n/a
Pitcher, 1 1/2 qt. covered _____ $250-300
Pitcher, redesigned _____ n/a
Plate, 6" B&B _____ $5-7
Plate, 7" salad _____ $15-18
Plate, 9" lunch _____ $10-12
Plate, 10" dinner _____ $25-30
Plate, 14" chop _____ $100-125
Plate, party w/ cup indent _____ $100-125
Plate, underplate for gravy _____ $15-18
Platter, 10" individual _____ n/a
Platter, 13" oval _____ $40-45
Platter, 15" oval _____ $40-45
Salt/Pepper stacking _____ $40-45
Salt and Pepper Mill _____ n/a
Sugar, original stack _____ $20-25
Sugar, family stack _____ n/a
Sugar, redesigned covered _____ n/a
Teapot, redesigned _____ n/a

Cookware

Dutch Oven, 6 qt., covered _____ n/a
Frypan, covered _____ n/a
Saucepan, covered _____ n/a
Warming Tray _____ n/a

Sugar White

Bowl, cereal	$15-18
Bowl, fruit original	$18-20
Bowl, fruit redesigned	$20-25
Bowl, deep soup	$50-60
Bowl, gumbo	$70-80
Bowl, 8" open vegetable	$60-70
Bowl, 10" serving bowl	$65-75
Butter dish, original	$125-150
Butter dish, redesigned	$500-600
Carafe	$250-275
Casserole, 2 qt. covered	$65-75
Casserole, 4 qt. covered	$150-175
Casserole, divided covered	$65-75
Coffeepot/Teapot covered	$150-175
Coffeepot AD covered	$125-150
Covers for soup/cereal & gravy	$15-20
Creamer, original	$15-20
Creamer, large family	$45-50
Creamer, redesigned	$45-50
Cup/Saucer original	$10-12
Cup/Saucer redesigned	$10-12
Cup/Saucer, coffee	$20-22
Cup/Saucer, after dinner	$125-150
Gravy, redesigned	$350-375
Gravy, attached stand	$100-125
Mug, original	$125-150
Mug, redesigned/tall coffee	$90-100
Pitcher, 1 1/2 qt. covered	$200-225
Pitcher, redesigned	$350-375
Plate, 6" B&B	$4-6
Plate, 7" salad	$12-15
Plate, 9" lunch	$25-30
Plate, 10" dinner	$20-25
Plate, 14" chop	$100-125
Plate, party w/ cup indent	$90-100
Plate, underplate for gravy	$15-20
Platter, 10" individual	$125-150
Platter, 13" oval	$40-50
Platter, 15" oval	$50-60
Salt/Pepper stacking	$40-45
Salt and Pepper Mill set	$750-850
Sugar, original stack	$20-25
Sugar, family stack	$65-75
Sugar, redesigned covered	$45-55
Teapot, redesigned	$250-275

Cookware

Dutch Oven, 6 qt., covered	$325-350
Frypan, covered	$250-275
Saucepan, covered	$250-275
Warming Tray	$2000+

Avocado Yellow, Parsley Green, and Ripe Apricot

Avocado Yellow and Ripe Apricot are beautiful earth tones that work well with many of the early colors of the line. Avocado was transformed from Chartreuse Yellow of the early raindrop period, into a smooth yellow/green glaze reminiscent of the inside of an avocado—not the dark green skin of the fruit. This color, along with Nutmeg Brown, has a wide variety of shades. Matching covers with bases, sugars with creamers, and stacking salt and peppers can be difficult.

Parsley Green is one of the most beautiful and popular colors of the line. Like Oyster, it had a short production run, resulting in several scarce pieces, such as the carafe, coffee mugs, and gumbos. Prices for this color are in general quite high, with certain pieces being at extreme premiums.

Parsley bowls: 10" serving bowl $50-60, 5" cereal $15-18, original fruit $12-15, gumbo $125-150, deep soup $60-70, 8" open vegetable $50-60. Avocado bowls: 10" serving $25-30, 5" cereal $8-10, original fruit $8-10, gumbo $30-35, deep soup $25-30, 8" open vegetable $25-30. Ripe Apricot bowls: 10" serving bowl $30-35, 5" cereal $8-10, original fruit $8-10, gumbo $30-35, deep soup $25-30, 8" open vegetable $25-30.

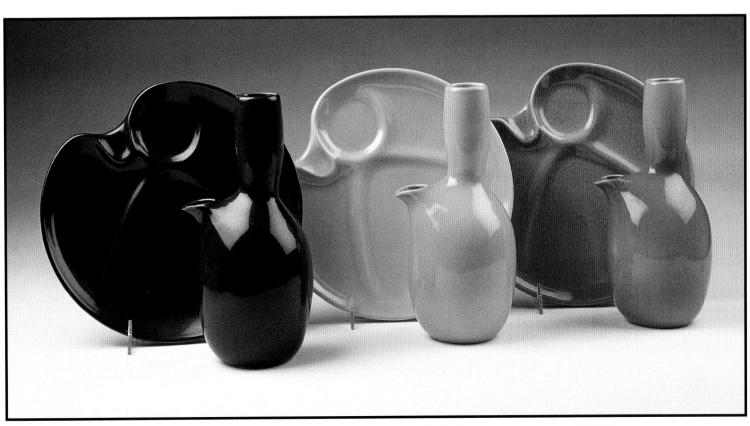

Parsley party plate $125-150, Parsley carafe (scarce) $400-450, Avocado party plate $65-75, Avocado carafe $150-175, Ripe Apricot party plate $50-60, Ripe Apricot carafe $150-175.

Covered pitchers: Parsley $200-225, Avocado $135-150, Ripe Apricot $125-135.

Close-up of party plates cup ring and finger holder.

Ripe Apricot redesigned butter $275-300, Parsley stacking salt and pepper $40-45, avocado original covered butter $65-75, Avocado gumbo $30-35, Ripe Apricot gumbo $30-35, Parsley gumbo $125-150.

Stacking sugars and creamers: Parsley $40-45 set, Avocado $25-30, Ripe Apricot $25-30. Two-quart casseroles: Parsley $50-60, Avocado $30-35, Ripe Apricot $30-35. Two-quart casseroles and divided vegetables are very slow sellers.

Platters: small Ripe Apricot (rare) $75-85, medium Avocado $20-25, large Parsley $45-50.

Parsley covered divided vegetable $40-45, Avocado chop plate $30-35, Ripe Apricot covered frypan $200-225.

Ripe Apricot redesigned c/s $8-10, Parsley early coffee c/s $12-15, Ripe Apricot original c/s $6-8, Parsley original c/s $10-12, Avocado AD coffeepot $75-85.

Avocado eggcup $35-40, Parsley covered pitcher $200-225, Parsley 10" dinner plate $20-25, Ripe Apricot lunch $12-15, Parsley 7" salad plate $15-18, Avocado 6" bread and butter plate $3-4.

Ripe Apricot original mug $90-100, Avocado demitasse c/s $100-125, Parsley original mug $175-200, Ripe Apricot demitasse c/s $100-125, Avocado original mug $100-125.

Ripe Apricot: dutch oven $250-275, covered frypan $200-225, covered saucepan $200-225.

Ripe Apricot: redesigned creamer $20-25, teapot $150-175, covered sugar $20-25.

Ripe Apricot: original mug $90-100, original c/s $6-8, redesigned mug $65-75, restyled c/s $8-10.

Ripe Apricot: salt and pepper mill $400-450 set, dutch oven $250-275, saucepan $200-225, frypan $200-225, party plate $50-60.

Ripe Apricot three-piece gravy $50-60, Parsley carafe $400-450, Ripe Apricot redesigned gravy $250-275, Parsley salt and pepper $40-45.

Parsley 4-qt. casserole $150-200, Ripe Apricot three-piece gravy $50-60, Avocado 2-qt. casserole $30-35.

Parsley original fruit $12-15, Ripe Apricot redesigned fruit $10-12.

Original Iroquois advertisement.

Iroquois backstamp.

Avocado family sugar $50-60, Avocado family creamer $30-35, Parsley sugar and creamer $40-45

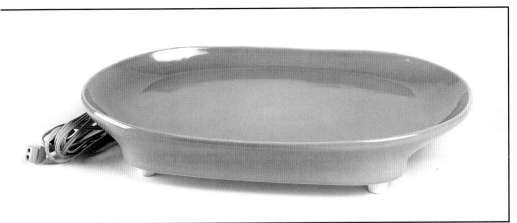

Electric warming tray.
Extremely rare, $1500-2000.

Advertisement for Iroquois
cookware. Depicts the warming
tray and an electric cooking unit.
This cooking unit has not been
reported.

Avocado Yellow (Chartreuse)

Bowl, cereal	$8-10
Bowl, fruit original	$8-10
Bowl, fruit redesigned	$10-12
Bowl, deep soup	$25-30
Bowl, gumbo	$30-35
Bowl, 8" open vegetable	$25-30
Bowl, 10" serving bowl	$25-30
Butter dish, original	$65-75
Butter dish, redesigned	n/a
Carafe	$150-175
Casserole, 2 qt. covered	$30-35
Casserole, 4 qt. covered	$75-100
Casserole, divided covered	$30-35
Coffeepot/Teapot covered	$175-200
Coffeepot AD covered	$75-85
Cover for soup/cereal & gravy	$12-15
Creamer, original	$12-15
Creamer, large family	$30-35
Creamer, redesigned	n/a
Cup/Saucer original	$8-10
Cup/Saucer redesiged	$10-12
Cup/Saucer, coffee	$8-10
Cup/Saucer, after dinner	$100-125
Gravy, redesigned	$275-300
Gravy, attached stand	n/a
Mug, original	$100-125
Mug, redesigned/tall coffee	n/a
Pitcher, 1 1/2 qt. covered	$135-150
Pitcher, redesigned	n/a
Plate, 6" B&B	$3-4
Plate, 7" salad	$8-10
Plate, 9" lunch	$12-15
Plate, 10" dinner	$8-10
Plate, 14" chop	$30-35
Plate, party w/ cup indent	$65-75
Plate, underplate for gravy	$12-15
Platter, 10" individual	n/a
Platter, 13" oval	$20-25
Platter, 15" oval	$25-30
Salt/Pepper stacking	$20-25
Salt and Pepper Mill	n/a
Sugar, original stack	$12-15
Sugar, family stack	$50-60
Sugar, redesigned covered	n/a
Teapot, restyled	$150-175

Cookware

Dutch Oven, 6 qt., covered	n/a
Frypan, covered	n/a
Saucepan, covered	n/a
Warming Tray	n/a

Ripe Apricot

Bowl, cereal	$8-10
Bowl, fruit original	$8-10
Bowl, fruit redesigned	$10-12
Bowl, deep soup	$25-30
Bowl, gumbo	$30-35
Bowl, 8" open vegetable	$25-30
Bowl, 10" serving bowl	$30-35
Butter dish, original	$65-75
Butter dish, redesigned	$275-300
Carafe	$150-175
Casserole, 2 qt. covered	$30-35
Casserole, 4 qt. covered	$75-85
Casserole, divided covered	$25-30
Coffeepot/Teapot covered	n/a
Coffeepot AD covered	$75-85
Covers for soup/cereal & gravy	$10-15
Creamer, original	$8-10
Creamer, large family	n/a
Creamer, redesigned	$20-25
Cup/Saucer original	$6-8
Cup/Saucer redesigned	$8-10
Cup/Saucer, coffee	n/a
Cup/Saucer, after dinner	$100-125
Gravy, redesigned	$250-275
Gravy, attached stand	$65-75
Mug, original	$90-100
Mug, redesigned/tall coffee	$65-75
Pitcher, 1 1/2 qt. covered	$125-135
Pitcher, redesigned	$275-300
Plate, 6" B&B	$2-3
Plate, 7" salad	$6-8
Plate, 9" lunch	$12-15
Plate, 10" dinner	$8-10
Plate, 14" chop	$35-40
Plate, party w/ cup indent	$50-60
Plate, underplate for gravy	$10-12
Platter, 10" individual	$75-85
Platter, 13" oval	$20-25
Platter, 15" oval	$25-30
Salt/Pepper stacking	$20-25
Salt and Pepper Mill set	$400-450
Sugar, original stack	$15-20
Sugar, family stack	n/a
Sugar, redesigned covered	$20-25
Teapot, redesigned	$150-175

Cookware

Dutch Oven, 6 qt., covered	$250-275
Frypan, covered	$200-225
Saucepan, covered	$200-225
Warming Tray	$1500-2000

Parsley Green

Bowl, cereal _____ $15-18
Bowl, fruit original _____ $12-15
Bowl, fruit redesigned _____ n/a
Bowl, deep soup _____ $60-70
Bowl, gumbo _____ $125-150
Bowl, 8" open vegetable _____ $50-60
Bowl, 10" serving bowl _____ $50-60
Butter dish, original _____ $125-150
Butter dish, redesigned _____ n/a
Carafe _____ $400-450
Casserole, 2 qt. covered _____ $50-60
Casserole, 4 qt. covered _____ $150-200
Casserole, divided covered _____ $40-45
Coffeepot/Teapot covered _____ n/a
Coffeepot AD covered _____ $125-150
Covers for soup/cereal & gravy _____ $15-18
Creamer, original _____ $15-20
Creamer, large family _____ n/a
Creamer, redesigned _____ n/a
Cup/Saucer original _____ $10-12
Cup/Saucer redesigned _____ n/a
Cup/Saucer, coffee _____ $12-15
Cup/Saucer, after dinner _____ $200-250
Gravy, redesigned _____ n/a
Gravy, attached stand _____ n/a
Mug, original _____ $175-200
Mug, redesigned/tall coffee _____ n/a
Pitcher, 1 1/2 qt. covered _____ $200-225
Pitcher, redesigned _____ n/a
Plate, 6" B&B _____ $4-6
Plate, 7" salad _____ $15-18
Plate, 9" lunch _____ $12-15
Plate, 10" dinner _____ $20-25
Plate, 14" chop _____ $100-125
Plate, party w/ cup indent _____ $125-150
Plate, underplate for gravy _____ $12-15
Platter, 10" individual _____ n/a
Platter, 13" oval _____ $35-40
Platter, 15" oval _____ $45-50
Salt/Pepper stacking _____ $40-45
Salt and Pepper Mill _____ n/a
Sugar, original stack _____ $20-25
Sugar, family stack _____ n/a
Sugar, redesigned covered _____ n/a
Teapot, redesigned _____ n/a

Cookware

Dutch Oven, 6 qt., covered _____ n/a
Frypan, covered _____ n/a
Saucepan, covered _____ n/a
Warming Tray _____ n/a

Nutmeg Brown and Lemon Yellow

Nutmeg Brown was in production longer than any other color except ice blue. The early brown is the least mottled of the four original colors. It tends to be foamy and very heavy. Nutmeg came into the line in 1947 (in a foamy glaze) and was in production until 1964. This glaze varies greatly. It is one of the least sought after of the Casual colors.

Lemon Yellow is extremely popular because it mixes well with both the earth tones and the pastels. It was produced in the late 1950s and early 1960s. Several variant shades exist for Lemon Yellow.

Nutmeg redesigned pitcher $275-300, Nutmeg covered pitcher $125-150, Lemon Yellow covered divided vegetable $40-50, Nutmeg redesigned c/s $8-10.

Nutmeg 4-qt. casserole $100-125, Lemon carafe $225-250, Nutmeg redesigned creamer $20-25, Nutmeg redesigned covered sugar $20-25.

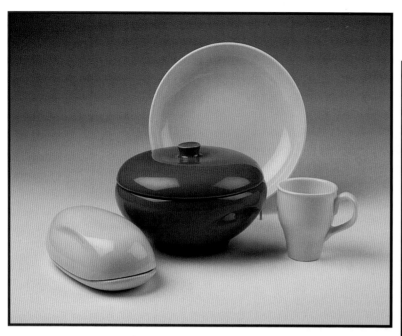

Lemon butter $80-100, Nutmeg redesigned 2-qt. casserole $30-35, Lemon 10" serving bowl $40-45, Lemon redesigned mug $75-85.

Nutmeg carafe $150-175, Lemon medium platter $25-30 Nutmeg covered cereal $20-22.

Nutmeg chop plate $40-45, Lemon 10" dinner plate $12-15, Nutmeg 9" lunch plate $10-12, Lemon 7" salad plate $10-12, Nutmeg 6" bread and butter plate $3-4.

Lemon Yellow: pepper mill $275-300, redesigned fast stand gravy $65-75, redesigned covered gravy (mushroom shaped) $275-300, saucepan $250-275.

Lemon teapot $175-200, Lemon stacking sugar and creamer $25-30, Nutmeg redesigned creamer $20-25, Nutmeg redesigned sugar $20-25.

Lemon stacking creamer $10-15, Nutmeg stacking sugar $10-15, Lemon redesigned creamer (front) $25-30, Nutmeg stacking creamer $10-15, Lemon stacking sugar $15-20, Nutmeg redesigned sugar $20-25.

Clockwise from left: Lemon gumbo $35-40, Nutmeg divided vegetable $20-25, Nutmeg 10" serving bowl $25-30, Lemon 5" cereal $12-15, Lemon fruit $10-12, Nutmeg redesigned fruit $10-12, Nutmeg fruit $8-10.

Nutmeg: covered butter $60-70, AD coffeepot $75-85, stacking sugar and creamer $25-30, AD c/s $100-125, stacking salt and pepper $20-25, original c/s $6-8.

Nutmeg original mug $90-100, Lemon redesigned mug $75-85, Nutmeg original c/s $6-8, Lemon restyled c/s $10-12, Nutmeg AD c/s $100-125.

Nutmeg Brown

Bowl, cereal	$8-10
Bowl, fruit original	$8-10
Bowl, fruit redesigned	$10-12
Bowl, deep soup	$25-30
Bowl, gumbo	$35-40
Bowl, 8" open vegetable	$25-30
Bowl, 10" serving bowl	$25-30
Butter dish, original	$60-70
Butter dish, redesigned	n/a
Carafe	$150-175
Casserole, 2 qt. covered	$30-35
Casserole, 4 qt. covered	$100-125
Casserole, divided covered	$25-30
Coffeepot/Teapot covered	$100-125
Coffeepot AD covered	$75-85
Cover for soup/cereal	$10-12
Creamer, original	$10-15
Creamer, large family	$30-35
Creamer, redesigned	$20-25
Cup/Saucer original	$6-8
Cup/Saucer redesigned	$8-10
Cup/Saucer, coffee	$6-8
Cup/Saucer, after dinner	$100-125
Gravy, redesigned	$275-325
Gravy, attached stand	$75-85
Mug, original	$90-100
Mug, redesigned/tall coffee	$50-60
Pitcher, 1 1/2 qt. covered	$125-150
Pitcher, redesigned	$275-300
Plate, 6" B&B	$3-4
Plate, 7" salad	$8-10
Plate, 9" lunch	$10-12
Plate, 10" dinner	$8-10
Plate, 14" chop	$40-45
Plate, party w/ cup indent	$50-60
Plate, underplate for gravy	$10-12
Platter, 10" individual	n/a
Platter, 13" oval	$20-22
Platter, 15" oval	$25-30
Salt/Pepper stacking	$20-25
Salt and Pepper Mill set	$450-500
Sugar, original stack	$10-15
Sugar, family stack	$40-50
Sugar, redesigned covered	$20-25
Teapot, redesigned	$175-200

Cookware

Dutch Oven, 6 qt., covered	$225-250
Frypan, covered	$175-225
Saucepan, covered	$200-225
Warming Tray	????

Lemon Yellow

Bowl, cereal	$12-15
Bowl, fruit original	$10-12
Bowl, fruit redesigned	$12-15
Bowl, deep soup	$30-35
Bowl, gumbo	$35-40
Bowl, 8" open vegetable	$30-35
Bowl, 10" serving bowl	$40-45
Butter dish, original	$80-100
Butter dish, redesigned	$350-400
Carafe	$225-250
Casserole, 2 qt. covered	$40-45
Casserole, 4 qt. covered	n/a
Casserole, divided covered	$40-50
Coffeepot/Teapot covered	n/a
Coffeepot AD covered	n/a
Cover for soup/cereal & gravy	n/a
Creamer, original	$10-15
Creamer, large family	n/a
Creamer, redesigned	$25-30
Cup/Saucer original	$8-10
Cup/Saucer redesigned	$10-12
Cup/Saucer, coffee	n/a
Cup/Saucer, after dinner	n/a
Gravy, redesigned	$275-300
Gravy, attached stand	$65-75
Mug, original	$100-125
Mug, redesigned/tall coffee	$75-85
Pitcher, 1 1/2 qt. covered	$175-200
Pitcher, redesigned	$300-350
Plate, 6" B&B	$2-3
Plate, 7" salad	$10-12
Plate, 9" lunch	$20-25
Plate, 10" dinner	$12-15
Plate, 14" chop	$40-50
Plate, party w/ cup indent	n/a
Plate, underplate for gravy	n/a
Platter, 10" individual	$80-100
Platter, 13" oval	$25-30
Platter, 15" oval	$30-35
Salt/Pepper stacking	$22-25
Salt and Pepper Mill set	$550-600
Sugar, original stack	$15-20
Sugar, family stack	n/a
Sugar, redesigned covered	$20-25
Teapot, restyled	$175-200

Cookware

Dutch Oven, 6 qt., covered	$225-275
Frypan, covered	$200-225
Saucepan, covered	$250-275
Warming Tray	????

Lettuce Green, Ice Blue, and Pink Sherbet

The four pastel colors (the fourth being lemon yellow) look great together, but also can work with other colors in the line. Lettuce is extremely popular at the moment and commands a premium price. Blue is also popular but there is also a great supply as this color was produced longer than any other color in the line. The early powder blue is a different shade of blue and tends to be foamy. Pink Sherbet is currently the least favored of these colors.

Pink Sherbet redesigned pitcher $300-325, Blue chop plate $45-50, Lettuce carafe $400-450, Blue stacking sugar and creamer $20-25.

Lemon Yellow 2-qt. redesigned casserole $40-45, Blue medium platter $20-25, Lettuce redesigned gravy $350-400, Blue redesigned sugar $25-30, Blue redesigned creamer $20-25, Lettuce stacking salt and pepper $30-35.

Pink redesigned mug $50-60, Lettuce original mug
$175-200, Blue AD c/s $100-125.

Blue redesigned gravy $250-275,
Lemon redesigned fast stand gravy
$65-75, Pink three-piece original gravy
$50-60.

Lettuce 4-qt. casserole $140-160, Pink original 2-qt. casserole
$30-35, blue redesigned 2-qt. casserole $40-45.

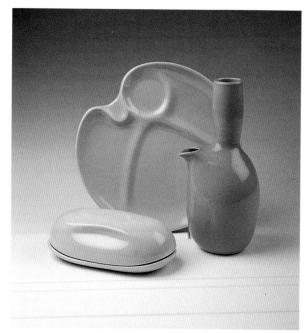

Pink party plate $50-60, Blue carafe
$175-200, Lettuce butter $90-100.

Lettuce: teapot $250-275, redesigned creamer $30-35, redesigned sugar $30-35, redesigned cup/saucer $10-15.

Medium platters: Pink $20-25, Blue $20-25, Lemon $25-30. Redesigned mugs: Pink $50-60, Lettuce $100-125, Blue $60-70.

Pink pepper mill $275-300, Lettuce dutch oven $400-450, Pink saucepan $225-250, Blue frypan $225-250.

Lettuce redesigned c/s $10-15, Blue AD c/s $100-125, Pink original c/s $8-10.

Blue party plate $60-70, Lettuce covered pitcher $225-250, Pink stacking sugar and creamer $25-30.

Blue AD coffeepot $85-95, Pink AD c/s $100-125.

Blue redesigned divided casserole $30-35, Pink original divided casserole $30-35, Pink redesigned divided casserole $30-35, Blue original divided casserole $30-35.

Pink bowls, clockwise from left: gumbo $35-40, 10" serving bowl $40-45, 8" open vegetable $30-35, redesigned fruit $12-15, original fruit $8-10, 5" cereal $10-12, (center) deep soup $30-35.

Saucepans: Blue $200-225, Lemon $225-250, Pink $225-250. Lettuce salt and pepper $30-35.

Blue saucepan $200-225, original store sign $35-45.

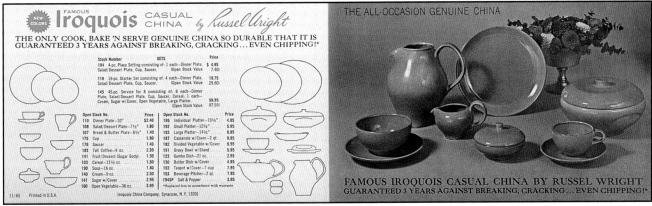

Original Iroquois pamphlet with prices. $50-60.

Lettuce Green

Bowl, cereal	$12-15
Bowl, fruit original	$10-12
Bowl, fruit redesigned	$15-18
Bowl, deep soup	$40-45
Bowl, gumbo	$65-75
Bowl, 8" open vegetable	$40-45
Bowl, 10" serving bowl	$55-65
Butter dish, original	$90-100
Butter dish, redesigned	$400-500
Carafe	$400-450
Casserole, 2 qt. covered	$50-60
Casserole, 4 qt. covered	$140-160
Casserole, divided covered	$50-60
Coffeepot/Teapot covered	n/a
Coffeepot AD covered	???
Cover for soup/cereal & gravy	$18-20
Creamer, original	$20-25
Creamer, large family	n/a
Creamer, redesigned	$30-35
Cup/Saucer original	$10-12
Cup/Saucer redesigned	$10-15
Cup/Saucer, coffee	n/a
Cup/Saucer, after dinner	$150-175
Gravy, redesigned	$350-400
Gravy, attached stand	$100-125
Mug, original	$175-200
Mug, redesigned/tall coffee	$100-125
Pitcher, 1 1/2 qt. covered	$225-250
Pitcher, redesigned	$450-500
Plate, 6" B&B	$3-4
Plate, 7" salad	$12-15
Plate, 9" lunch	$25-30
Plate, 10" dinner	$15-18
Plate, 14" chop	$75-100
Plate, party w/ cup indent	$90-100
Plate, underplate for gravy	$20-25
Platter, 10" individual	$125-150
Platter, 13" oval	$30-35
Platter, 15" oval	$40-45
Salt/Pepper stacking	$30-35
Salt and Pepper Mill set	$600-800
Sugar, original stack	$20-25
Sugar, family stack	n/a
Sugar, redesigned covered	$30-35
Teapot, restyled	$250-275

Cookware

Dutch Oven, 6 qt., covered	$400-450
Frypan, covered	$300-325
Saucepan, covered	$325-350
Warming Tray	????

Ice Blue

Bowl, cereal	$8-10
Bowl, fruit original	$8-10
Bowl, fruit redesigned	$10-12
Bowl, deep soup	$25-30
Bowl, gumbo	$35-40
Bowl, 8" open vegetable	$25-30
Bowl, 10" serving bowl	$30-35
Butter dish, original	$60-70
Butter dish, redesigned	$325-350
Carafe	$175-200
Casserole, 2 qt. covered	$40-45
Casserole, 4 qt. covered	$75-100
Casserole, divided covered	$30-35
Coffeepot/Teapot covered	$125-150
Coffeepot AD covered	$85-95
Cover for soup/cereal & gravy	$12-15
Creamer, original	$8-10
Creamer, large family	$25-35
Creamer, redesigned	$20-25
Cup/Saucer original	$6-8
Cup/Saucer redesigned	$8-10
Cup/Saucer, coffee	$6-8
Cup/Saucer, after dinner	$100-125
Gravy, redesigned	$250-275
Gravy, attached stand	$65-75
Mug, original	$90-100
Mug, redesigned/tall coffee	$60-70
Pitcher, 1 1/2 qt. covered	$125-150
Pitcher, redesigned	$250-275
Plate, 6" B&B	$3-4
Plate, 7" salad	$8-10
Plate, 9" lunch	$12-15
Plate, 10" dinner	$10-12
Plate, 14" chop	$45-50
Plate, party w/ cup indent	$60-70
Plate, underplate for gravy	$12-15
Platter, 10" individual	$70-80
Platter, 13" oval	$20-25
Platter, 15" oval	$25-30
Salt/Pepper stacking	$20-25
Salt and Pepper Mill set	$500-600
Sugar, original stack	$10-15
Sugar, family stack	$40-50
Sugar, redesigned covered	$25-30
Teapot, redesigned	$175-200

Cookware

Dutch Oven, 6 qt., covered	$200-225
Frypan, covered	$225-250
Saucepan, covered	$200-225
Warming Tray	???

Pink Sherbet

Bowl, cereal	$10-12
Bowl, fruit original	$8-10
Bowl, fruit redesigned	$12-15
Bowl, deep soup	$30-35
Bowl, gumbo	$35-40
Bowl, 8" open vegetable	$30-35
Bowl, 10" serving bowl	$40-45
Butter dish, original	$70-80
Butter dish, redesigned	$275-325
Carafe	$175-200
Casserole, 2 qt. covered	$30-35
Casserole, 4 qt. covered	$80-100
Casserole, divided covered	$30-35
Coffeepot/Teapot covered	n/a
Coffeepot AD covered	$85-100
Covers for soup/cereal & gravy	$10-15
Creamer, original	$8-10
Creamer, large family	n/a
Creamer, redesigned	$20-25
Cup/Saucer original	$8-10
Cup/Saucer redesigned	$8-10
Cup/Saucer, coffee	n/a
Cup/Saucer, after dinner	$100-125
Gravy, redesigned	$250-275
Gravy, attached stand	$60-65
Mug, original	$100-125
Mug, redesigned/tall coffee	$50-60
Pitcher, 1 1/2 qt. covered	$175-200
Pitcher, redesigned	$300-325
Plate, 6" B&B	$2-3
Plate, 7" salad	$8-10
Plate, 9" lunch	$15-18
Plate, 10" dinner	$8-10
Plate, 14" chop	$40-45
Plate, party w/ cup indent	$50-60
Plate, underplate for gravy	$10-15
Platter, 10" individual	$100-125
Platter, 13" oval	$20-25
Platter, 15" oval	$30-35
Salt/Pepper stacking	$20-25
Salt and Pepper Mill set	$550-600
Sugar, original stack	$15-20
Sugar, family stack	n/a
Sugar, redesigned covered	$20-25
Teapot, redesigned	$175-200

Cookware

Dutch Oven, 6 qt., covered	$225-250
Frypan, covered	$225-250
Saucepan, covered	$225-250
Warming Tray	????

Cantaloupe, Brick Red, Aqua, and Mustard Gold

Redesigned pitchers: Brick Red $1800-2000, Aqua $2000-2500, Cantaloupe $1200-1500.

The later colors are the most rare of the Casual Line. Cantaloupe was produced for only four years. It is found in sufficient quantity to put a set together. Brick Red, Aqua Blue (called turquoise in company literature), and Mustard Gold, on the other hand, were produced for less than two years and are very difficult to find. Mustard Gold does not command the extremely high prices of Aqua and Brick Red, but is also difficult to find.

Serving pieces in Brick Red and Aqua are heavily prized by Russel Wright collectors. But as with any collectible, only so many people are willing to pay the really high prices. We have tried to average prices, but in many cases we know of Aqua and Brick Red pieces selling for extremely high prices. Aqua stacking salt and peppers recently sold for over $1000 on eBay™, and Aqua teapots have sold for as much as $3500. Whether these prices can be sustained is a question we cannot answer.

Cantaloupe stacking sugar and creamer $125-150. set, Aqua chop plate $300-350, Brick Red redesigned creamer $150-175, Brick Red redesigned sugar $175-200.

Cantaloupe 10" dinner plate $25-30, Aqua 7" salad plate $50-60, Brick Red 6" bread and butter plate $30-35, Brick Red c/s $60-70, Aqua c/s $75-85, Cantaloupe c/s $20-25.

Brick Red divided casserole $200-225, Aqua 2-qt. casserole $300-350, Cantaloupe divided casserole $175-200.

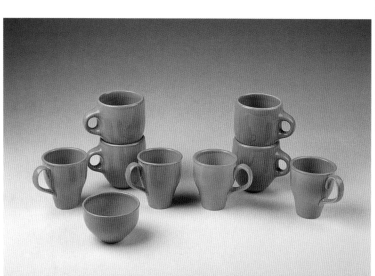

Cantaloupe redesigned mug $175-200, original mug $225-250, handleless cup $75-100.

Cantaloupe medium platter $100-125, Aqua large platter $250-275, Brick Red fast stand gravy $225-250.

Redesigned butters: Aqua $1500-2000, Brick Red $1400-1600, Mustard Gold $350-400.

Aqua redesigned sugar $200-250, teapot $1800-2000, creamer $200-250.

Cantaloupe redesigned gravy $1500-1800.

Clockwise from left: Brick Red 8" vegetable $175-200, Cantaloupe 10" serving bowl $125-150, Cantaloupe gumbo $125-150, Cantaloupe fruit $30-35, Brick Red redesigned fruit $45-50, Cantaloupe 5" cereal $25-30. Center: Aqua deep soup $175-200.

Cantaloupe divided casserole $175-200, 2-qt. casserole $200-225, frypan $800-1000.

Redesigned creamers: Cantaloupe $80-100, Aqua $200-250, Brick Red $150-175.

Cantaloupe salt and pepper mill $1800-2000.

Aqua pitcher $2000-2500, 2-qt. casserole $300-350, divided casserole $300-325.

Bowls, front to back: Aqua redesigned fruit $65-75, cereal $75-85, deep soup $175-200. Cantaloupe redesigned fruit $30-35, cereal $25-30, deep soup $100-125. Brick Red redesigned fruit $45-50, cereal $75-85, 8" vegetable $175-200.

Cantaloupe redesigned sugar $75-100, teapot $1000-1200, redesigned creamer $80-100.

Aqua large platter $250-275, Cantaloupe original butter $250-300, Brick Red redesigned butter $1400-1600.

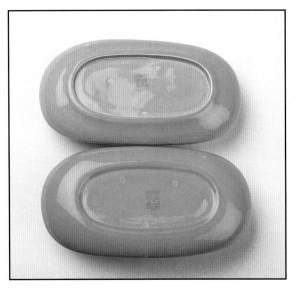

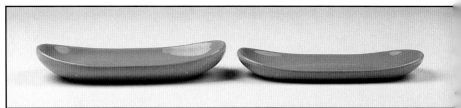

Mold variations of butter bottoms.

Aqua redesigned butter $1500-2000.

Redesigned mugs Brick Red $250-275, Aqua $250-275, Cantaloupe $175-200.

Mustard Gold fast stand gravy $100-125, Aqua pitcher $2000-2500, Mustard Gold 2-qt. casserole $75-100, Aqua redesigned butter $1500-2000.

Cantaloupe bowls, clockwise from left: 8" vegetable $100-125, 10" serving bowl $125-150, gumbo $125-150, fruit $30-35, redesigned fruit $30-35, cereal $25-30. Center: deep soup $100-125.

Cantaloupe salt and pepper $125-150 set, Brick Red salt and pepper $250-300, Cantaloupe salt and pepper mill $1800-2000 set.

Cantaloupe bowls. Bowls on the left are redesigned, and those on right are the original shape. Notice the more defined foot on the redesigned bowls.

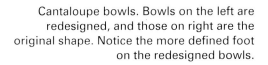

Original Iroquois pamphlet with prices. $50-60.

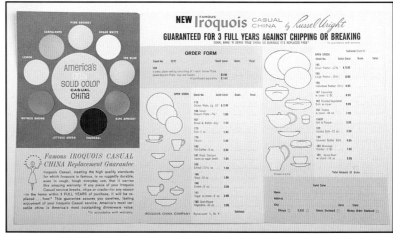

Cantaloupe: 10" individual platter $200-250, 14" chop plate $250-275, large platter $125-150, medium platter $100-125.

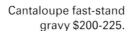

Cantaloupe fast-stand gravy $200-225.

Cantaloupe

Bowl, cereal	$25-30
Bowl, fruit original	$30-35
Bowl, fruit redesigned	$30-35
Bowl, deep soup	$100-125
Bowl, gumbo	$125-150
Bowl, 8" open vegetable	$100-125
Bowl, 10" serving bowl	$125-150
Butter dish, original	$250-300
Butter dish, redesigned	n/a
Carafe	$1000-1200
Casserole, 2 qt. covered	$200-225
Casserole, 4 qt. covered	n/a
Casserole, divided covered	$175-200
Coffeepot/Teapot covered	n/a
Coffeepot AD covered	n/a
Cover for soup/cereal	n/a
Creamer, original	$50-60
Creamer, large family	n/a
Creamer, redesigned	$80-100
Cup/Saucer original	n/a
Cup/Saucer redesigned	$20-25
Cup/Saucer, coffee	n/a
Cup/Saucer, after dinner	n/a
Gravy, redesigned	$1500-1800
Gravy, attached stand	$200-250
Mug, original	$225-250
Mug, redesigned/tall coffee	$175-200
Pitcher, 1 1/2 qt. covered	???
Pitcher, redesigned	$1200-1500
Plate, 6" B&B	$15-18
Plate, 7" salad	$20-25
Plate, 9" lunch	$40-45
Plate, 10" dinner	$25-30
Plate, 14" chop	$250-275
Plate, party w/ cup indent	n/a
Plate, underplate for gravy	n/a
Platter, 10" individual	$200-250
Platter, 13" oval	$100-125
Platter, 15" oval	$125-150
Salt/Pepper stacking	$125-150
Salt and Pepper Mill set	$1800-2000
Sugar, original stack	$75-90
Sugar, family stack	n/a
Sugar, redesigned covered	$75-100
Teapot, redesigned	$1000-1200

Cookware

Dutch Oven, 6 qt., covered	$600-800
Frypan, covered	$800-1000
Saucepan, covered	$800-1000
Warming Tray	???

Brick Red

Bowl, cereal $75-85
Bowl, fruit original .... n/a
Bowl, fruit redesigned $45-50
Bowl, deep soup $150-175
Bowl, gumbo $200-225
Bowl, 8" open vegetable $175-200
Bowl, 10" serving bowl .... n/a
Butter dish, original .... n/a
Butter dish, redesigned $1400-1600
Carafe .... n/a
Casserole, 2 qt. covered $400-450
Casserole, 4 qt. covered .... n/a
Casserole, divided covered $200-225
Coffeepot/Teapot covered .... n/a
Coffeepot AD covered .... n/a
Cover for soup/cereal .... n/a
Creamer, original .... n/a
Creamer, large family .... n/a
Creamer, redesigned $150-175
Cup/Saucer original .... n/a
Cup/Saucer redesigned $65-75
Cup/Saucer, coffee .... n/a
Cup/Saucer, after dinner .... n/a
Gravy, redesigned .... n/a
Gravy, attached stand $225-250
Mug, original .... n/a
Mug, redesigned/tall coffee $250-275
Pitcher, 1 1/2 qt. covered .... n/a
Pitcher, redesigned $1800-2000
Plate, 6" B&B $30-35
Plate, 7" salad $50-60
Plate, 9" lunch .... n/a
Plate, 10" dinner $75-85
Plate, 14" chop .... n/a
Plate, party w/ cup indent .... n/a
Plate, underplate for gravy .... n/a
Platter, 10" individual $225-250
Platter, 13" oval $175-200
Platter, 15" oval $200-225
Salt/Pepper stacking $250-300
Salt and Pepper Mill .... n/a
Sugar, original stack .... n/a
Sugar, family stack .... n/a
Sugar, redesigned covered $175-200
Teapot, redesigned $1500-2000

Cookware
Dutch Oven, 6 qt., covered .... n/a
Frypan, covered .... n/a
Saucepan, covered .... n/a
Warming Tray .... n/a

Aqua (Turquoise)

Bowl, cereal	$75-85
Bowl, fruit original	n/a
Bowl, fruit redesigned	$65-75
Bowl, deep soup	$175-200
Bowl, gumbo	$200-225
Bowl, 8" open vegetable	$175-200
Bowl, 10" serving bowl	n/a
Butter dish, original	n/a
Butter dish, redesigned	$1500-2000
Carafe	n/a
Casserole, 2 qt. covered	$300-350
Casserole, 4 qt. covered	n/a
Casserole, divided covered	$300-325
Coffeepot/Teapot covered	n/a
Coffeepot AD covered	n/a
Cover for soup/cereal	n/a
Creamer, original	n/a
Creamer, large family	n/a
Creamer, redesigned	$200-250
Cup/Saucer original	n/a
Cup/Saucer redesigned	$75-85
Cup/Saucer, coffee	n/a
Cup/Saucer, after dinner	n/a
Gravy, redesigned	n/a
Gravy, attached stand	$300-325
Mug, original	n/a
Mug, redesigned/tall coffee	$250-275
Pitcher, 1 1/2 qt. covered	n/a
Pitcher, redesigned	$2000-2500
Plate, 6" B&B	$30-35
Plate, 7" salad	$50-60
Plate, 9" lunch	n/a
Plate, 10" dinner	$75-85
Plate, 14" chop	n/a
Plate, party w/ cup indent	n/a
Plate, underplate for gravy	n/a
Platter, 10" individual	$400-450
Platter, 13" oval	$225-250
Platter, 15" oval	$250-275
Salt/Pepper stacking	$600-700
Salt and Pepper Mill	n/a
Sugar, original stack	n/a
Sugar, family stack	n/a
Sugar, redesigned covered	$200-250
Teapot, restyled	$1800-2000

Cookware

Dutch Oven, 6 qt., covered	n/a
Frypan, covered	n/a
Saucepan, covered	n/a
Warming Tray	n/a

Mustard Gold

Bowl, cereal _____ $12-15
Bowl, fruit original _____ n/a
Bowl, fruit redesigned _____ $18-20
Bowl, deep soup _____ $40-45
Bowl, gumbo _____ $50-60
Bowl, 8" open vegetable _____ $35-40
Bowl, 10" serving bowl _____ n/a
Butter dish, original _____ n/a
Butter dish, redesigned _____ $350-400
Carafe _____ n/a
Casserole, 2 qt. covered _____ $75-100
Casserole, 4 qt. covered _____ n/a
Casserole, divided covered _____ $40-50
Coffeepot/Teapot covered _____ n/a
Coffeepot AD covered _____ n/a
Cover for soup/cereal _____ n/a
Creamer, original _____ n/a
Creamer, large family _____ n/a
Creamer, redesigned _____ $30-35
Cup/Saucer original _____ n/a
Cup/Saucer redesigned _____ $10-12
Cup/Saucer, coffee _____ n/a
Cup/Saucer, after dinner _____ n/a
Gravy, redesigned _____ n/a
Gravy, attached stand _____ $100-125
Mug, original _____ n/a
Mug, redesigned/tall coffee _____ $100-125
Pitcher, 1 1/2 qt. covered _____ n/a
Pitcher, redesigned _____ $350-400
Plate, 6" B&B _____ $4-5
Plate, 7" salad _____ $10-12
Plate, 9" lunch _____ n/a
Plate, 10" dinner _____ $12-15
Plate, 14" chop _____ n/a
Plate, party w/ cup indent _____ n/a
Plate, underplate for gravy _____ n/a
Platter, 10" individual _____ $100-125
Platter, 13" oval _____ $30-35
Platter, 15" oval _____ $40-45
Salt/Pepper stacking _____ $35-45
Salt and Pepper Mill _____ n/a
Sugar, original stack _____ n/a
Sugar, family stack _____ n/a
Sugar, redesigned covered _____ $35-40
Teapot, redesigned _____ $200-225

Cookware

Dutch Oven, 6 qt., covered _____ n/a
Frypan, covered _____ n/a
Saucepan, covered _____ n/a
Warming Tray _____ n/a

Additional Casual Items, Including Prototypes

Avocado coffeepot with early mottled glaze, $175-200. Extremely rare Blue tall coffee—only two known. Coffeepot is *not* marked. $2000-2500.

Large coffeepot with handled gravy. Gravy was purchased with large coffeepot in large set. The color is definitely the same as the rest of the set. Probably not a Russel Wright design.

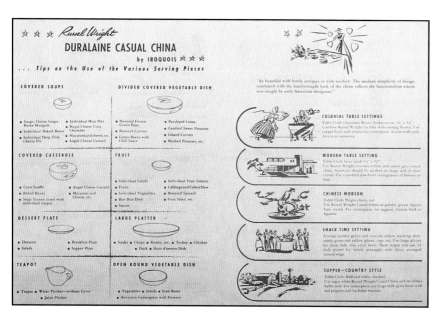

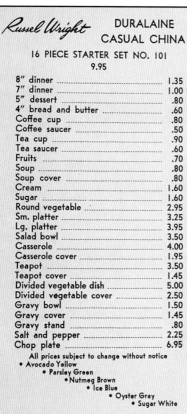

Iroquois pamphlet for "Duralaine Casual". The Duralaine name seems to have been dropped very early in the line, in favor of simply "casual."

Iroquois eggcups, $40-50. These eggcups are found in at least five of the Russel Wright Iroquois glazes. They are probably not a Russel Wright design, but make a great addition to the dinnerware line.

Foamy Avocado covered cereal, $30-35
Covered coffeepot, $175-200.

Handleless cups. These are redesigned cups without the handles. Pink $40-50, White $50-60, Charcoal $50-60, Ripe Apricot $40-50, Cantaloupe $100-125, Lettuce $60-70.

Parsley chop plate. Decorated stacking sugar and creamer $40-50, covered cereal $20-25.

Shepherd's Purse: 8" vegetable $20-25, 10" dinner $10-12, 6" bread and butter plate $4-5, redesigned sugar $20-25, redesigned creamer plain $20-25, cup and saucer $8-10.

Woodhue: 10" dinner plate $25-30, cup and saucer $12-15.

Gay Wings medium platter $25-30.

Pepper Tree medium platter $25-30.

White Violets: 8" vegetable $20-25, 10" dinner plate $10-12, 6" bread and butter plate $4-5, cup and saucer $8-10.

Original Iroquois pamphlet with prices. $80-100

Experimental redesigned teapot in glaze close to the color of Seafoam. NV.

Cover to saucepan with confetti overglaze. Cantaloupe over Lemon Yellow. Unfortunately the base was broken in the mail. NV

Experimental glazes and molds for 8" open vegetable. $75-100 each.

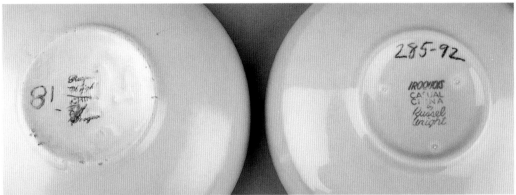

10" dinner plate in experimental light Oyster glaze. Marked with test numbers $50-75.

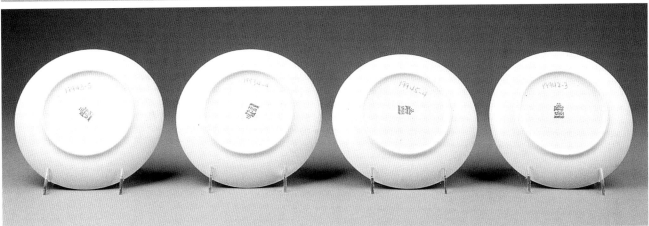

Test glazes for 6" plates. $40-50 each

Charcoal 17" meat platter. (12" wide) Russel Wright
glaze color, but probably not his design. $100-150

Prototype casserole with warming stand. Part of a large set found in Syracuse. Documentation of these pieces as Russel Wright's designs are in the Syracuse archive. NV

1952 Christmas ashtray. Depicts man juggling Russel Wright dishes. $200-225.

Four styles of Russel Wright cups—from earliest to latest. Blue thick coffee cup, Oyster coffee cup, Ripe Apricot original cup, Cantaloupe redesigned cup.

Sterling China

Russel Wright's designs for Sterling China were an attempt to create a dinnerware line that would appeal both to retail and institutional customers. This was attractive to Wright, for it enabled a high volume of sales to a new group of customers. Similarly, it was attractive to Sterling for enabling them to enter the home market while adding an air of prestige to their institutional lines.

Russel Wright's designs for Sterling were done in 1949. The only piece in the line that was restyled was the pitcher, which was simply too large and heavy for restaurant use. The resulting change was one of Russel Wright's perfect designs. The restyled water pitcher is both beautiful and functional—and highly sought after today.

Russel Wright presented five glazes for use with this line: Ivy Green, Straw Yellow, Cedar Brown, Suede Grey, and Shell Pink. In addition, stock White was used. Shell Pink and undecorated White dinnerware were produced in smallest quantity and are considered scarce today.

Sterling China's contract with Russel Wright allowed them to use his shapes with added decorations for the institutional lines. He was still paid a royalty, but less than what he was paid if his glazes were also used. The variety of decorations on this dinnerware is extensive, from simple leaves to cowboys roping a cow. These were done by Sterling artists, not Russel Wright.

Russel Wright also worked with Sterling on the development of dishes for the Shun Lee Dynasty restaurant in New York. Wright was working on an overall concept for the design of the restaurant and incorporated Sterling for the dinnerware. The resulting line was called Polynesian. Although most of the pieces were made for this one specific restaurant, enough pieces have turned up in remote locations to indicate that at least some was sold to other restaurants or as novelty dishes.

Restyled pitchers: Cedar brown $175-200, Straw Yellow $175-200, Ivy Green $225-250, Pink $300-325

Original pitchers: Cedar Brown
$125-150, Straw Yellow $100-125,
Suede Grey $125-150, Ivy Green
$140-160.

Comparison of original and restyled pitchers.

Straw Yellow restyled pitcher
$175-200.

Plates: Straw 11" service plate $18-20, Cedar Brown 10" dinner $15-18, Grey 9" lunch plate $14-16, Ivy 7" salad plate $10-12, Pink 6" bread and butter $8-10.

Clockwise from back: Ivy Green divided relish $100-125. Ashtrays, Grey $75-85, White $100-125, Ivy $75-85, Straw $60-70. Individual creamers, Grey $12-15, Straw $10-12, Ivy $12-15. Straw pickle, $20-25.

Individual teapots: Ivy $125-150, Cedar Brown $100-125, Pink $175-200, Straw $100-125, Grey $125-150, White $140-160.

Cups and saucers: regular Straw $15-18, regular Pink $20-25, Ivy demitasse $75-100, Cedar demitasse $65-75.

Platters: Ivy 7" $20-22, Grey 10 1/2" $20-25, Straw 11 3/4" $18-20, Pink 13 1/2" $40-45.

Coffee bottles: Cedar Brown $100-125, Grey $125-150, Straw $100-125.

Clockwise from left: Straw coffee bottle $100-125, Ivy original pitcher $140-160, grey covered sugar $25-30, Pink demitasse c/s $175-200, Ivy 1-oz. creamer $12-15, Straw 3-oz. creamer $10-12, Cedar Brown sauceboat $30-35, White teapot (center) $140-160.

Ivy teapot $125-150, coffee bottle $125-150, AD c/s $75-100

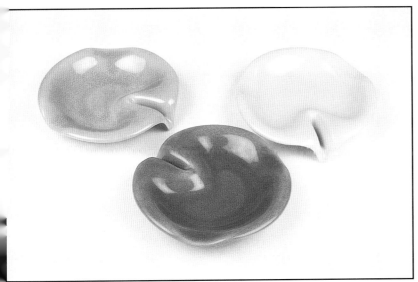

Sterling ashtrays: Grey $75-85, Straw $60-70, experimental brown glaze $125-150.

Bowls: Grey 5" fruit $10-12, Straw 7-oz. bouillon, $18-20, 6 1/2" Grey soup $15-18, Straw 7 1/2" salad $20-22.

Ivy: 1-oz. creamer $12-15, 3-oz. $15-18. Butter pat or underplate for 1-oz. creamer. Matches both in glaze and style, but unlisted in any company literature. NV

Backstamp for Sterling China.

Rubber backstamp for Sterling China. Rare. NV

Straw Yellow: 7 1/2" salad bowl $20-22, 10" dinner $15-18, 7" salad plate $10-12, coffee bottle $100-125, 1-oz. creamer $10-12, regular c/s $15-18, 5" fruit $8-10.

Several pieces from the Warhol collection. These pieces bring premium prices because of the Warhol label. Expect to pay $20-50 extra for pieces with a label.

Decorated Sterling dinner plate with covered wagon scene. $35-40

Decorated 11" serving plate from Harold's Club Reno. $50-60

Decorated dinner plate from Harman's Ranch. $25-30

Decorated dinner plate with cowboy scene. $30-35

Sterling decorated with black leaves. Values 10% to 20% less than non-decorated pieces.

Decorated pitchers $75-100 each.

Decorated teapot $50-75.

Floral decorations.

Decorated with grapes. Pitcher
$125-150, cup/saucer $10-12,
plate $10-12.

Decorated Sterling with brown flowers. Brown glaze matches
Cedar Brown pieces. 10%-20% lower than undecorated Sterling.

Decorated with pink flowers.
Cup restyled into mug. Mug/
saucer $15-20, platter $15-20.

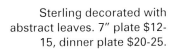

Sterling decorated with
abstract leaves. 7" plate $12-
15, dinner plate $20-25.

Polynesian. Rice bowl $50-60, Coffeepot $200-250.

Palm king saucer $8-10, teapot with brown trim (no cover) $15-20.

Backstamp for Polynesian pieces.

Coffeepot $200-250, 12" chop $50-75, fish platter $100-125.

Sake bottle $200-300, 12" chop $50-75.

14" chop, $75-100.

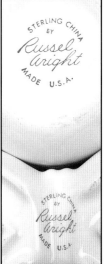

Backstamps on benefit pieces.

New Sterling pieces made for benefit auction. Maroon coffee bottle (no cover was made 1998) $75-100, butterfly dish (1997) $30-40, teapot $75-100. These pieces are marked Russel Wright. We have not seen any documentation to indicate that Russel Wright designed the butterfly, but it is possible that this was executed from a design that was made during the original production.

Highlight

Highlight was produced by Paden City in the early 1950s. While negotiations and contracts started in the late 1940s, it appears that the dinnerware did not make it to stores until a couple of years later. Wright and his distributor Justin Tharaud seem to have equally large egos and appear to have gotten in each other's way much to the detriment of the production and distribution of the product. This, paired with the financial problems at Paden City Pottery and Paden City Glass Co., resulted in a line that was virtually doomed from the start.

Despite the problems, Highlight is a beautiful and elegant line of dinnerware. First produced in Citron, Pepper, Nutmeg, and Blueberry, the dishes are extremely popular with collectors, but are somewhat impractical for regular use. These dishes chip. Underside nicks are regularly found on pieces that look like they have never been used.

Clockwise from left: Citron oval platter $40-50, Nutmeg chop plate $50-55, Citron dinner $20-25, Nutmeg 6" plate $8-10, Citron creamer $25-30, Citron covered vegetable $125-150, Nutmeg dinner $20-25.

Similarly, the beautiful Snow Glass accessories, made by Paden City Glass are especially prone to small hairline cracks. Collecting this pattern is further complicated by the fact that these dishes were produced in both a matte and a high gloss glaze. The two styles do not mix well.

In addition to the four basic colors, White and Medium Green were added late in the run. Very little of these two later colors seems to have been produced.

Dinner plates: Dark Green $40-45, Citron $20-25, Pepper $25-30, Nutmeg $20-25. White 6" plate $12-15, Pepper covered sugar $65-75.

Blueberry round vegetable $40-50, Pepper platter $60-65, Blueberry cereal $25-30, Citron creamer $25-30, Pepper creamer $30-35, White covered sugar $65-75, Pepper salt and pepper (Very rare) $1000-1200.

Salt and pepper, $1000-1200.

Pepper and Snow Glass. Pepper oval vegetable $60-65, Snow Glass cover to vegetable $500-600, Snow Glass large tumbler $225-250, Snow Glass 8" plate $100-125, pepper sugar base $30-35, Snow Glass sugar cover $200-250, pepper cup $20-25, Snow Glass saucer $75-100, pepper salt and pepper $1000-1200, Snow Glass small tumbler $200-225, Snow Glass fruit bowl $150-175.

Creamers: Blueberry $30-35, Dark green $60-65, Nutmeg $25-30, Pepper $30-35.

Blueberry fruit bowl $22-25, Nutmeg cup $18-20, White saucer $10-12, White fruit $25-28.

Pepper cup $20-25, Snow Glass saucer $75-100, Snow Glass pitcher (Very rare) $1500-2000, Pepper creamer $30-35.

Snow Glass pitcher, $1500-2000.

  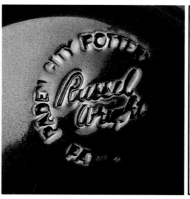 

Different backstamps and labels for Highlight.

 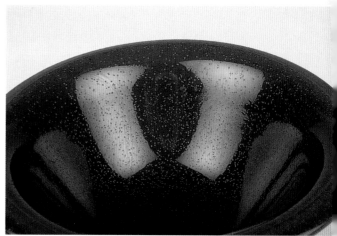

Blueberry round vegetable with odd speckled glaze. $100-150

Original photo from Russel Wright archive of Highlight and Snow Glass, with three sizes of tumblers and very rare vegetable bowl. Snow Glass vegetable $700-800. *Courtesy of Syracuse University Library, Special Collections.*

Harker White Clover

Russel Wright's White Clover dinnerware was his first full-scale attempt to integrate pattern into a dinnerware design. Produced by the Harker China Company in 1951, the line contained a simple dinner service with a few serving pieces. Most pieces were decorated with a White Clover design, yet plates were originally produced without decoration. This was altered early in the production.

The line was produced in four colors: Golden Spice, Meadow Green, Coral Sand, and Charcoal. Charcoal is the current favorite, followed closely by Meadow Green. The undecorated General Electric clock was one of the most heavily advertised of any Russel Wright design. Unfortunately, the rest of the line was not well marketed. The 1950s were a difficult time for Ohio potters, and distribution for this line relied heavily on Russel Wright.

This dinnerware is somewhat scarce today. Despite claims that the line was craze-proof and chip-resistant, the line's raised edge frequently chipped or bruised. The solid white covers of the pitcher and casseroles are very difficult to find in good condition.

Spice covered casserole $100-125, Charcoal 13" platter $40-45, Coral covered pitcher $125-150, Green gravy $40-45.

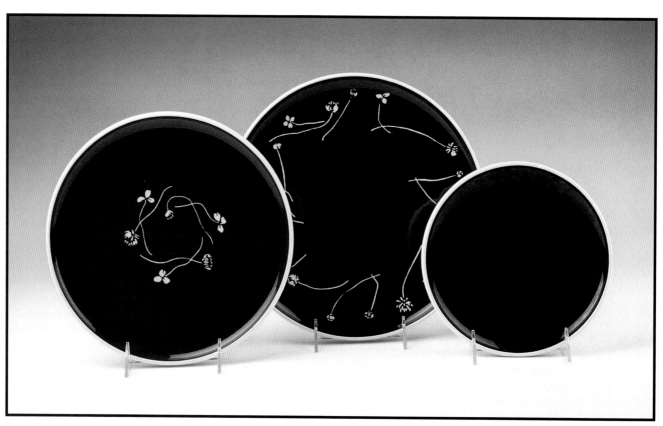

Charcoal plates: 9" decorated dinner $15-18, 11" decorated chop $35-40, 7" salad plate $10-12.

Charcoal covered vegetable $90-100, Spice divided vegetable $100-125, Coral covered casserole $100-125, Green ashtray $35-40.

Undecorated plates: 10" Charcoal dinner $18-20, 9" Green dinner $12-15, 7" Charcoal salad $10-12, 6" Green bread and butter $4-5, Charcoal creamer $20-25

Original magazine ad.

Covered pitchers: Spice $125-150, Charcoal $150-175, Coral $125-150.

Charcoal: fruit dish (decorated inside) $10-12, cereal (decorated outside) $18-20, cup and saucer $12-15, 9" dinner $15-18.

Green cup and saucer $10-12, Spice covered pitcher $100-125, Coral salt and Spice pepper $30-35 set, Charcoal creamer $20-25, Green sugar $30-35.

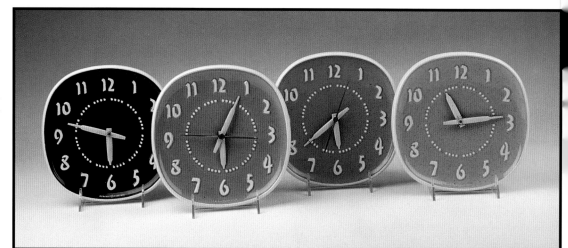

General Electric clocks: Charcoal $90-100, Coral, Green, and Spice. $70-80 each.

Divided vegetable. White with decorations $100-125, Spice $100-125.

Ad for Harker GE clocks. There seems to be more advertisements for these clocks than for any other Russel Wright designs.

9" Spice plate with decorations for St. Anthony's Church. $30-35.

Magazine ad for White Clover.

AFTER THE BALL GAME IS OVER, set your supper right out on a football field such as this one. Give your imagination free play to make the most of your very best beans and a huddle of hot dogs. The goal post is made from 1½ x 1½ wood strips perched at a jaunty angle and flanked by a grandstand of chrysanthemums. Yard lines of tape are placed over a dark brown or green cloth. To win that extra point, mold an edible football—your favorite cream-cheese spread shaped like a pigskin and laced with pimiento strips. A neat buffet trick is the placing of napkins to make serving still simpler. The dinnerware here is bright in color, and it is plastic and virtually unbreakable

PARTY PRETTY AT ANY MEAL is Russell Wright's dinnerware with an incised pattern that never, never wears off. Pieces are ovenproof, and shaped for easy stacking and chip prevention. Such charcoal and white pottery looks smart as all get-out if you carry through with black and white mats—has a whole new personality if you use colored linens for contrast.

BEWITCHING WITCH, at right, is a sweetheart in disguise. Her head's a popcorn ball, with licorice hair and jelly-bean eyes. A row of gum drops "button up" her black cloak.

Get Set for

70

Knowles Esquire

Knowles Esquire line was produced from 1955 to 1962. Seven patterns were produced, most in a distinct color. With the exception of Antique White, which is solid white, and Solar, each of these patterns reflect Russel Wright's interest in plants and nature.

Despite the simple elegance of this line, it was not the most practical line of dinnerware. It scratched very badly and the gold highlights washed off. It also cracked very easily. These problems, complicated by distribution nightmares, resulted in a line that simply could not succeed.

Because of the number of patterns, early attempts to make this dinnerware open stock failed. It was most frequently marketed in complete sets.

Grass 8" salad $12-15, Seeds 10" dinner $12-15, Queen Anne's Lace 6" bread and butter $5-8.

Seeds 6" soup/cereal $12-15, Antique White 10" dinner plate $20-22, Snowflower 5" fruit/dessert $8-10, Queen Anne's Lace cup and saucer $12-15, Grass cup and saucer $10-12.

Pitchers: Snowflower $125-150, Antique White $150-175, Grass $140-160.

Antique White: 4" x 6" sauceboat $75-100, pitcher $150-175, covered serving bowl $125-150, teapot $250-275.

Teapots: Seeds $175-200, Antique White $250-275, Botanica $250-300.

Seeds: oval vegetable $40-45, 14" large oval platter $35-40, open compote 7" x 12" $275-300, covered sugar $40-45, teapot $175-200.

Grass creamer $30-35, Seeds teapot $175-200, Queen Anne's Lace sugar bowl $40-45.

Solar creamer, $35-40. Solar teapot, $200-225.

Queen Anne's Lace divided vegetable $65-75.

Queen Anne's Lace: salt and pepper set $60-65, pitcher $140-160, creamer $30-35, sauceboat $50-60, covered sugar $40-45.

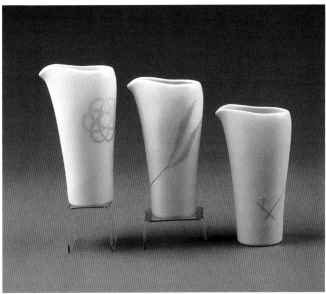

Creamers: Solar $40-45, Grass $30-35, Snowflower $30-35.

Solar 9" vegetable $50-60, Seeds 14" platter $35-40, Grass oval vegetable $50-60, Snowflower fruit $10-12, Seeds soup/cereal $12-15.

Platters: 13" Snowflower $30-35, Seeds 14" $35-40, Grass 13" $45-50.

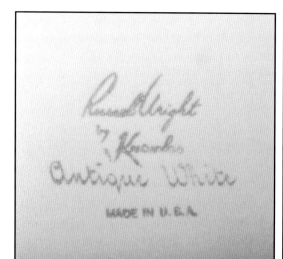

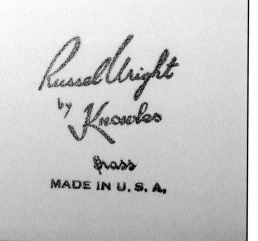

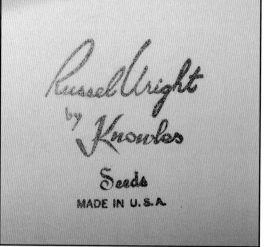

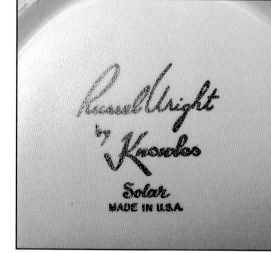

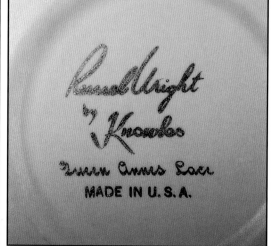

Backstamps for Knowles patterns.

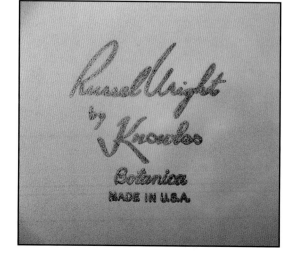

Plastic Dinnerware

Russel Wright's interest in plastic dinnerware dates from the mid-1940s and continued into the 1960s. At least five separate lines were produced starting with the Meladur line in the late 1940s.

Wright's most successful line was Residential by Northern. Made in a variety of colors in the 1950s, the line was expanded and altered later in the decade to include wonderfully textured colors and a variety of designs.

His Flair line from 1959 contains his most interesting plastic design. Several patterns were created in this line, including Ming Lace—an off-White plastic with actual leaves encased in the dinnerware. It remains extremely popular today.

Finally, in the early 1960s, Ideal produced a set of toy dishes that were exact replicas in miniature of American Modern. This set was extremely well marketed, sold in several large mail order catalogues. Many of these sets survive, and while they are cute, they are not highly sought after. They are pictured in the American Modern section of this book.

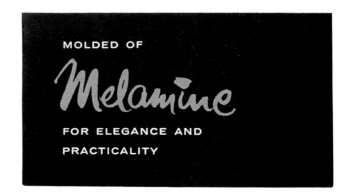

DINNERWARE BY

Russel Wright "RESIDENTIAL"

MOLDED OF

Melamine

FOR ELEGANCE AND PRACTICALITY

Residential brochure. $20-25

Residential dinnerware: Lug soups $5-7 each, cup/saucer $4-5, 6" plate $2-3, salad plate $4-5, dinner plate $5-6, confetti chop plate $20-25, covered sugar $50-55, creamer $12-15.

Red chop plate $15-20, Black Velvet covered vegetable $30-35, Black Velvet divided vegetable $20-25.

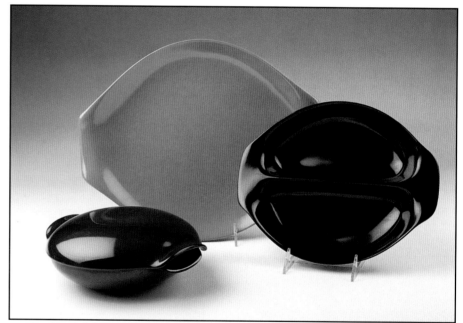

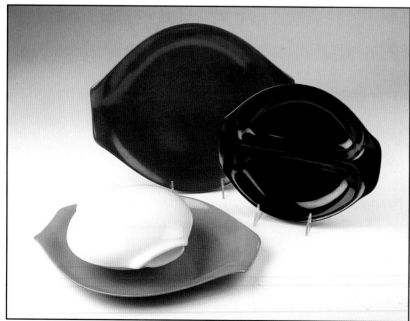

Copper chop plate $30-35, Black Velvet divided vegetable $20-25, Yellow covered vegetable $20-25, Red chop plate $15-20.

Melmac magazine advertisement that includes Residential dinnerware.

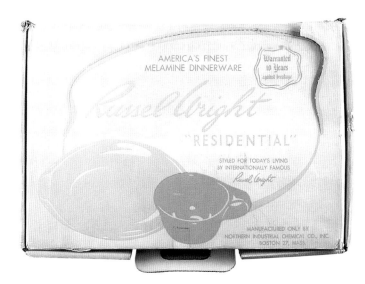

Residential boxed set. Scarce. $150-175.

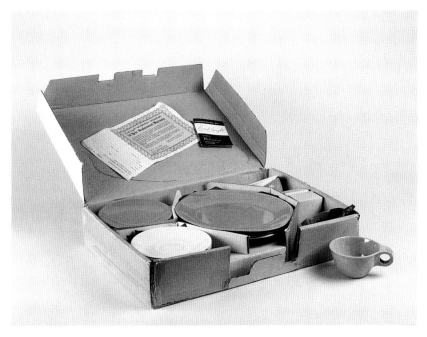

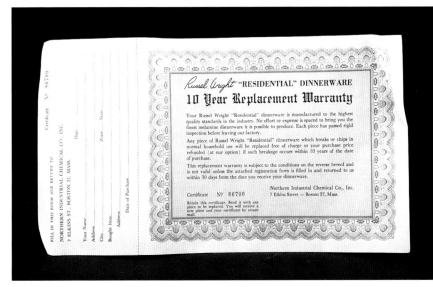

Original Residential warranty.

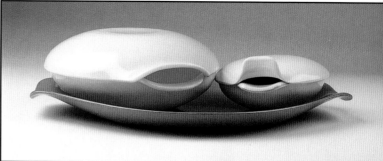

Yellow covered vegetable $20-25, covered soup $15-20, red chop plate $15-20.

Backstamp for Residential.

Covered soup $15-25, covered vegetable $20-35. Displayed on an inverted divided vegetable.

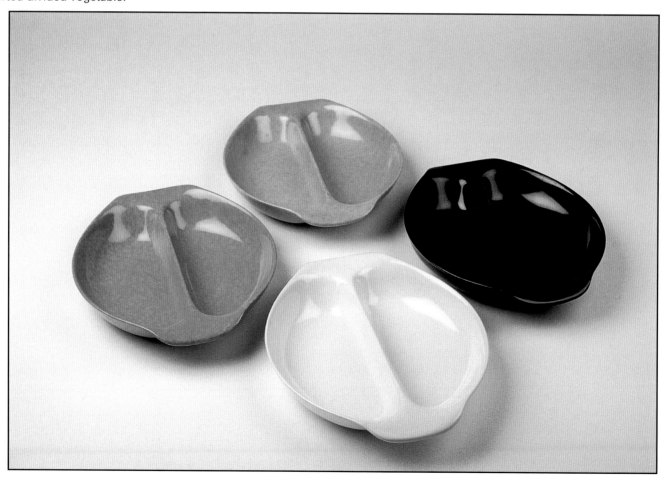

Divided vegetables: Grey $10-12, Black $20-25, Yellow $10-12, Blue $10-12.

Residential and Home Decorator dinnerware: patterned plates $4-5, creamer $10-12, cup/saucer $4-5, fruit bowl $5-6, small tumbler $10-12.

Backstamp for Home Decorators, Inc. plastic.

Flair patterned dinner plates: Spring Garden red, Spring Garden blue, and Golden Bouquet. $10-15 each

Magazine advertisement for Melmac dinnerware, including Residential.

Advertising brochures for Flair's patterned lines.

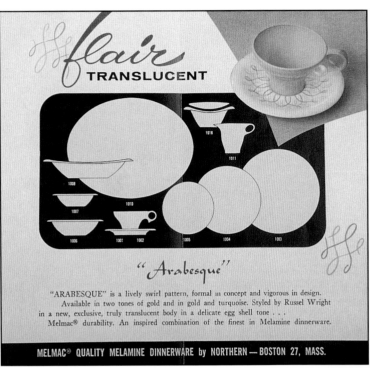

flair *by* NORTHERN BOSTON 27, MASS.

flair TRANSLUCENT — SPRING GARDEN

"Spring Garden"

1030-8 16 PC. STARTER SET FOR 4 (8 Pcs. Decorated) $12.95
(BLUE OR PINK)
Consists of 4 ea. #1001 Cups, #1002 Saucers, #1003 Dinner Plates and #1006 Soup-Cereal Bowls. Dinner Plates and Saucers in Blue or Pink Spring Garden Pattern on Eggshell White. Cups and Bowls in Eggshell White.

1045-17 45 PC. SERVICE FOR 8 (17 Pcs. Decorated) $34.50
(BLUE OR PINK)
Consists of 8 ea. #1001 Cups, #1002 Saucers, #1003 Dinner Plates, #1005 Bread and Butter Plates, #1006 Soup-Cereal Bowls and 1 ea. #1008 Vegetable Bowl, #1010 Platter, #1011 Creamer, #1018 Sugar Bowl, #1019 Sugar Cover. Dinner Plates, Saucers and Platter in Blue or Pink Spring Garden Pattern on Eggshell White. All Other Pieces in Eggshell White.

OPEN STOCK PRICES
NOTE: All Items Marked With Asterisk (*) Are Decorated As Priced Below.

1001	7 OZ. CUP	$1.50
1002	6" SAUCER*	1.50
1003	10" DINNER PLATE*	2.95
1004	8" SALAD-LUNCHEON PLATE*	1.95
1005	6" BREAD AND BUTTER PLATE*	1.00
1006	14 OZ. SOUP-CEREAL BOWL	1.25
1007	8 OZ. FRUIT-DESSERT BOWL	1.00
1008	24 OZ. VEGETABLE BOWL	3.00
1010	15" PLATTER*	4.50
1011	CREAMER	1.50
1018	SUGAR BOWL (With #1019 Cover)	1.75

All Decorated (*) Pieces in Blue or Pink Spring Garden Pattern on Eggshell White. Other Pieces Eggshell White, Turquoise or Pink.

DESIGNED BY *Russel Wright*

flair TRANSLUCENT

"Spring Garden"

"SPRING GARDEN" suggests the first delicate blossoms of Spring, expressed in soft blue or pink with gracefully entwined green stems. Styled by Russel Wright in a new, exclusive, truly translucent body in a delicate egg shell tone . . . Melmac® durability. An inspired combination of the finest in Melamine dinnerware.

MELMAC® QUALITY MELAMINE DINNERWARE by NORTHERN – BOSTON 27, MASS.

flair *by* NORTHERN BOSTON 27, MASS.

flair TRANSLUCENT — MING LACE LEAVES

"Ming Lace Leaves"

1030-16 16-PIECE STARTER SET FOR 4 (16 Pcs. Decorated) $16.95
Consists of 4 each #1001 Cups, #1002 Saucers, #1003 Dinner Plates and #1006 Soup-Cereal Bowls. In Jade or Bamboo. Real leaf decoration on Egg Shell ware.

1040-35 45-PIECE SERVICE FOR 8 (43 Pcs. Decorated) $49.95
Consists of 8 each #1001 Cups, #1002 Saucers, #1003 Dinner Plates, #1004 Salad-Luncheon Plates, #1006 Soup-Cereal Bowls and 1 each #1008 Vegetable Bowl, #1010 Platter, #1011 Creamer, #1018 Sugar Bowl and #1019 Sugar Bowl Cover. In Jade or Bamboo on Egg Shell White

OPEN STOCK PIECES
NOTE: All Items Marked With Asterisk (*) Are Decorated As Priced Below.

1001	8-OZ. CUP*	$1.50
1002	6" SAUCER*	1.50
1003	10" DINNER PLATE*	3.00
1004	8" SALAD-LUNCHEON PLATE*	2.25
1006	14-OZ. SOUP-CEREAL BOWL*	1.95
1007	8-OZ. FRUIT-DESSERT BOWL*	1.50
1008	24-OZ. VEGETABLE BOWL*	3.75
1010	15" PLATTER*	4.95
1011	CREAMER	1.50
1018	SUGAR BOWL (With #1019 Decorated Cover*)	2.25

DESIGNED BY *Russel Wright*

flair TRANSLUCENT

"Ming Lace Leaves"

"MING LACE LEAVES" are the actual leaves of the Jade Orchid Tree, imported from China. The Jade Orchid was originally cultivated in China during the Ming Dynasty. This rare and beautiful tree grows in the Orient to this very day. These are the actual leaves of the Jade Orchid Tree, cleaned of vegetation, tinted Jade (green), hand placed and permanently molded into fine translucent dinnerware.

MELMAC® QUALITY MELAMINE DINNERWARE by NORTHERN — BOSTON 27, MASS.

Pink Flair cup and saucer, $6-8. Green
Meladur cereal $10-12, fruit $5-6.

Backstamp for Meladur plastic.

Flair backstamp.

Flair Ming Lace: oval vegetable $20-25, 15" platter $30-35, 8" salad/luncheon plate $10-12, cup and saucer $10-12, covered sugar $30-35, creamer $15-18.

Ideal plastic: blue tumbler $15-20 each, covered pitcher $100-125, white juice tumblers in original package $25-30 each, three-piece salad set $75-100, covered butter $75-100.

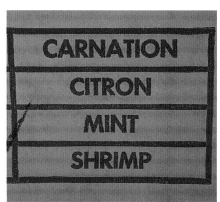

Side of Ideal box listing the names of the colors.

Beverage set with original box and labels, $200-225.

Original advertisement for Ideal Plastic.

Shinko Shikki plate $125-150, covered rice $150-175.

Sovereign Dinnerware

Russel Wright's Sovereign dinnerware is closely tied in shape to the Knowles line. Produced by the Canadian company in the late 1950s, very little is known about the extent of pieces produced, the colors, or its distribution. The Syracuse archives have virtually no information on this line.

The colors so far identified are Light Blue, Pink, and White. Each has a speckling reminiscent of Taylor, Smith and Taylor's Pebbleford line. In addition to pieces photographed, a salt and pepper shaker exists. Certainly there is more to this line.

Sovereign Potteries, Mary and Russel Wright dinnerware.

Covered sugar $75-100, oval serving dish $65-75, pink creamer $75-100.

Cup and saucer $45-50, dinner plate $40-50, salad plate $35-40, fruit bowl $25-30, flat soup bowl $50-75.

White cup and saucer $45-50, blue cup and saucer $45-50, pink creamer $75-100.

Theme Formal and Theme Informal

Russel Wright's final dinnerware line was planned to be one of his most comprehensive. Incorporating porcelain, stoneware, plastic, and glass, he designed two contrasting lines, Theme Formal and Theme Informal. This dinnerware was produced in 1965 by Yamato in Japan and imported by Schmid International.

Theme Formal is a beautiful white porcelain line with matching elegant glassware. Informal was produced in two colors: Dune, a tan glaze with large white splotches; and Ember, a brown glaze with orange accents. Informal had matching tumblers and glass plates, as well as a plastic line called Shinko Shikki.

Although this set was not heavily marketed, it was available at Japanese importers in New York. Enough has emerged to indicate that this was not simply produced as prototypes, as previously thought. We know of several sets that have been found. Similarly, the Formal glassware is expensive but not especially rare.

Theme Formal dinnerware and glassware.

Salad plate $100-125, dinner plate $125-150, 6" plate $50-75, AD c/s $200-225

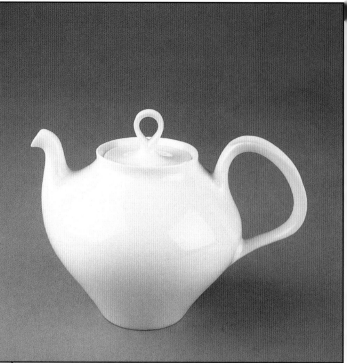

Teapot, $750-1000.

Backstamp of Theme Formal.

Theme Informal. Dune salad plate $75-100, Ember platter $350-400, Dune mug $175-200, Dune cup and saucer $100-150, Ember 6" plate $65-75, Dune cereal bowl $100-125.

Original label on Theme Formal glassware.

Theme Formal goblets. From left: water $150-175, wine $150-175, cocktail $125-150, cordial $200-225.

Dune saucer $40-50, dinner $100-125, salad $75-100.

Shinko Shikki covered rice bowl $150-175, Theme Informal tumbler $200-225, Shinko Shikki plate $125-150, Ember mug $175-200, Ember cup and saucer $100-150, Ember cereal $100-125.

Shinko Shikki backstamp $125-150, covered rice $150-175.

Theme Informal backstamp.

Ember mug $175-200, Dune creamer $250-275, Ember 6" plate $50-60, Ember cereal $100-125.

Mary Wright

Mary Wright's involvement in Russel's career should not be underestimated. In the early years, Mary acted as a sales representative and business manager. With Russel and Irving Richards, she formed Raymor, whose primary goal was to promote and distribute Russel's designs. Mary also provided much-needed capital for many of Russel's projects.

Mary's work as a designer dates to the mid-1930s. Like Russel, she designed wood serving pieces for Klise. She also worked with Raymond Loewy on aluminum pieces for the American Way line.

In 1946, Mary designed Country Garden for Bauer. The line, produced in beige, brown, pink, white, and green, consisted of a small dinner service with multi-purpose serving pieces. Its production was extremely limited. All examples of this line are considered rare and expensive.

Country Garden ladle $100-125, Mary Wright four-part wooden tray $300-350, pitcher $350-400, sauceboat/low pitcher $250-300, covered sugar (cover is sugar spoon) $225-250.

Salad plate $125-150, dinner plate $150-175,
cup and saucer $125-150.

Detail of cup and saucer. Notice
the convex saucer ring.

Ladle $100-125, salad plates
$125-150 each, Mary Wright
wooden tray $225-250, small
bowl $125-150.

Detail of sugar and spoon/cover.

Mary Wright wooden bowl $375-400, serving bowl $175-200, rectangular tray $150-175.

Backstamps for Country Garden pieces.

Ladles, $100-125 each.

Cruet with stopper. Rare, $350-375.

Small bowls $125-150 each, white skillet $250-275, ladle $100-125, oblong tray $175-200.

Covered sugar $225-250, creamer $175-200, oblong tray $175-200.

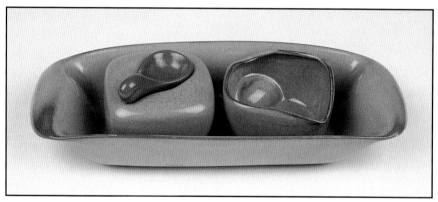

Cup and saucer $125-150 each set, dinner plate $150-175 each, serving bowl $175-200, creamer $175-200, covered sugar $225-250.

Bauer Pottery

Russel Wright's work with Bauer Pottery resulted in an incredible line of art pottery that is passionately collected today. The demand is so high for this pottery, with collectors of Bauer, Russel Wright, and general art pottery, that little is seen in the marketplace.

Produced for just over a year, 1945-1946, these designs are in extremely short supply. Most of the information that has emerged comes from thin files in the Syracuse archives that are often difficult to understand. This, paired with frequent errors in reference books, especially where photos are misidentified, has made it very difficult to unravel the extent of what was produced.

The core document in the Syracuse Archive is a typewritten list, with manuscript additions, of 21 items numbered 1A-22A (with no item listed for #10A). This chart lists item number, price ($1.25 to $10), a very brief description, main glazes (outside), and inside glazes. Only #1-20 have been previously identified. The price listed for both #21 and #22 is $1.25, the same price as the pinched ashtray #8. Having matched the colors on the list with actual examples, we believe #21 to be the folded ashtray, and #22 to be the 5″ ash bowl.

We have shown examples of each of these items in numerical order to help in the identification of these pieces. The aqua glaze is frequently confused with figured white. The aqua glaze appears as an off-white glaze with an aqua tint, not a strong blue like Iroquois aqua. Aqua pieces originally were 20% more expensive than the other colors. Trial glazes for many of these pieces have been found with test numbers, but no signature.

Bauer vases.

#1 Bauer Pillow vases.
$700-800 each

#2 8 1/2″ vases. From left: Atlanta Brick, Aqua, Jonquil Yellow, Figured White. $500-600 each

#3 Corsage vases.
$300-425 each

#3 Corsage vases. View from above.

Comparison of colors. From left: Figured White, Bubble White, Aqua.

#4 Jug vases. Clockwise from left: Bubble White, Jonquil Yellow, Aqua, Bubble White, and Atlanta Brick. $800-1000 each

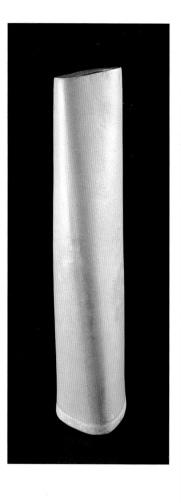

#5 Floor Vase. Extremely rare. $1800-2000

Two Jonquil Yellow #6 vases showing difference of glazing effects.

#6 10 1/2" vase oval. From left: Aqua, Jonquil Yellow, Georgia Brown, and Atlanta Brick. $650-800 each

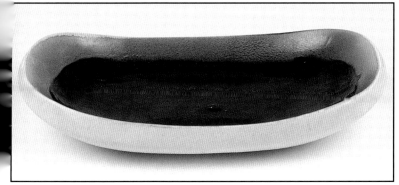

#7 Centerpiece bowl in Jonquil Yellow, 17" x 9". $700-800

#8 Pinch Ashtrays. $300-400 each

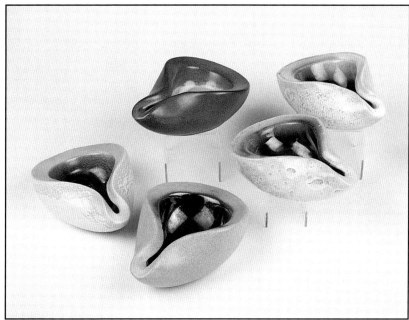

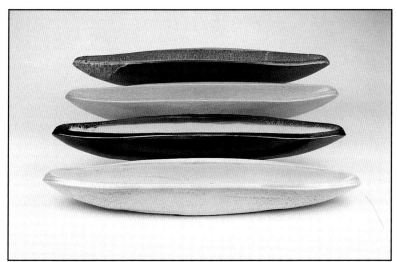

#9 Mantelpiece bowl. From front: Figured White, Gun Metal, Atlanta Brick, Georgia Brown. $800-1000 each

#11 Manta Ray bowl. From left. Experimental Green, Aqua, Gun Metal. $1200-1500 each

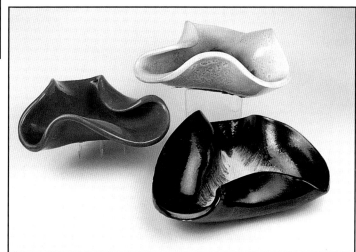

#12A 4 1/2" Square flower pot. Figured White, Georgia Brown, Atlanta Brick. $500-600 each

#13 7" Flower Pot, Atlanta Brick. This piece comes with a saucer/underplate. $600-700

Saucer/underplate for flower pot. Scarce. $400-500

#14 11" Candleholders. One in Georgia Brown and a pair in Aqua. $600-650 each

#15 Candleholder bowl, Figured White and Atlanta Brick. $800-1000

#16 Aqua 7 1/2" vase/flower pot. $800-900.

#17 Egg Yolk bowl. $500-600 each

#18 12" Tall vase. Jonquil Yellow, Aqua. $750-850 each

#19 Bulb bowls. $500-600 each

#20 Square vase, 20". Rare. $1000-1200

#21 Folded Ashtrays.
$300-400 each

#22 Square ashtrays.
$350-400 each

Comparison of glaze effects.

Collection of Bauer.

Russel Wright Aluminum

Russel Wright's first large line of consumer products was his spun aluminum. First created in his workshop, this line dates from 1930 and includes more than one hundred items. Most of these items were produced in limited quantity, yet some, like the round bun warmer, were produced in great number.

The aluminum line was divided into three categories: stove to tableware group, serving accessories group, and household items (lamps, vases, etc.). Many pieces incorporated other materials, like wooden knobs, brass handles, or Lucite trim.

The aluminum pieces scratched and dented easily. Customers were advised to use plain steel wool to remove scratches and keep the item bright. Most of the aluminum pieces that have survived are in fair condition. Prices should vary greatly depending on condition of the piece.

Photo of Russel Wright's showroom. *Courtesy Syracuse University Library, Special Collections.*

Spun Aluminum Punch set. $650-750

Bowl with bamboo handle $75-100, tumblers $15-20 each, ball pitcher with rattan on handle and foot $175-200, pitcher with wooden handle $75-100, tall pitcher with wooden ball as part of handle $200-225.

Spun Aluminum and cork cocktail set. $600-800.

Tall pitcher $200-225, tall vase $150-175, vegetable server and spoon $150-175.

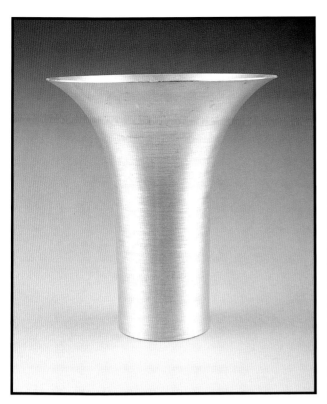

Tall vase, $150-175.

Small two-tiered aluminum and rattan server, $75-100. Large two-tiered server, $100-125. Bowl with wooden handle (high), $50-75. Bowl with wooden handle (low), $50-75.

Covered aluminum serving bowl $75-100, small covered cake $75-100, large covered cake $100-125.

Tea set with tray $250-300, pitcher with wooden handle $100-125, matching mugs $25-35 each.

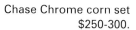

Chase Chrome corn set $250-300.

Covered gravy pan $65-75, copper ball vase $200-250, Plantene tumbler $75-100.

Photo from Russel Wright's showroom depicting Plantene and Oceana pieces.

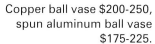

Copper ball vase $200-250, spun aluminum ball vase $175-225.

Ice bucket with wooden handle $50-60, Bun warmer with plastic handles $50-75, Bun warmer with wooden knob $50-75. The bun warmer with the wooden knob is the most frequently seen of all Russel Wright aluminum pieces. It is usually heavily scratched because of the way the top slides off of the base.

Serving tray with cork ball $90-110.

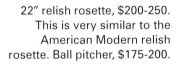

22″ relish rosette, $200-250. This is very similar to the American Modern relish rosette. Ball pitcher, $175-200.

Three-tiered vase $200-250, covered serving dish $100-125, small handled bowl $40-50.

Ice bucket/warming dish, $100-125. Bean pot with tray and serving spoon, $125-150.

Tray with glass insert, $75-100. Serving utensil, $75-100.

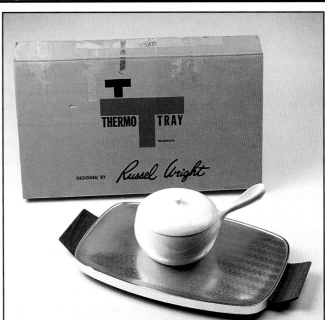

THERMO TRAY

DESIGNED BY *Russel Wright*

Electric "Thermo Tray" $60-80. These are relatively common. Box, $40-50.

Oceana and Other Wood

Mary and Russel Wright separately created numerous wooden items that today are extremely scarce. These items were first produced in Russel Wright's studio in the early 1930s. In 1935, Russel developed the Oceana line for the Klise Wood Working Company of Grand Rapids, Michigan. Working with beautiful hardwood—blonde maple, cherry, gum, and hazelwood—Russel was able to create items that seemed to be hand-carved. These marine-inspired creations combined exquisite grains with rich finishes.

Oceana pieces are marked with a burnt Russel Wright signature and can occasionally be found with an American Way paper label. Oceana was created as part of the American Way project.

Mary Wright pieces are similarly found with a burnt signature. All examples of Mary Wright's wooden creations are extremely rare.

Oceana salad bowl, $650-800.

Russel Wright signature backstamp of oceana salad bowl.

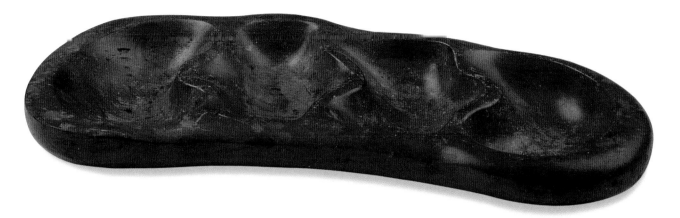

Oceana four-part relish, $500-600.

Russel Wright signature backstamp
and Oceana paper label.

Oceana salad bowl, $800-1000.

Oceana serving bowl , $750-850.

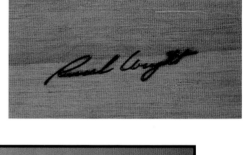

Backstamp of oceana serving bowl.

Oceana 7" bowl $350-400, Oceana 14" handled bowl/
tray $600-700, Oceana lazy susan $1000-1200.

Oceana: dark finish plate $200-250, light finish snail plate $300-350, 20" tray $700-800, 11" round bowl $750-850.

Mary Wright four-part serving tray, $350-400. Shown with American Modern Bean Brown shakers.

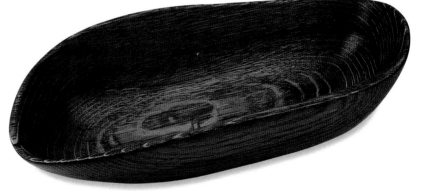

Mary Wright serving tray $300-350.

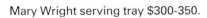

Mary Wright bowl $450-500.

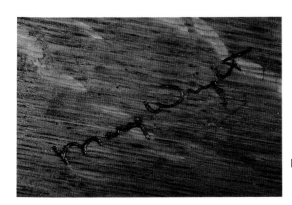

Mary Wright signature backstamp.

Russel Wright Glassware

Russel Wright Glassware

Russel Wright designed glassware for several glass companies in the 1950s and 1960s. Despite the production of a wide variety of lines, most of this glassware is scarce. Only the American Modern line, produced by Old Morgantown, and the Eclipse glassware, by Bartlett-Collins, are easily found.

Imperial's Pinch glassware is found in a variety of colors, in two distinct thicknesses. While the colors work well together, the two styles are incompatible. The thinner style seems to be more popular with collectors.

Imperial Glass Co. also produced Flair and Twist glassware. These items are extremely scarce. Flair comes in three sizes; Twist will be found in four sizes.

The Paden City Snow Glass pieces are among the most beautiful of Russel Wright's designs. Both tumblers and dinnerware were created, but it is extremely fragile and not much has survived.

The Yamato Theme Formal glassware, produced in 1965, is a beautiful opaline glass. Each piece has a unique iridescent quality. More of this glassware is being found than previously expected. It is expensive, but not rare.

Morgantown's American Modern Chartreuse. Back row: Pilsner $150-175, chilling bowl $125-150, chilling bowl insert/dessert bowl $40-50, double old-fashioned $75-85. Middle row: Goblet $20-25, wine $20-25, luncheon tumbler $18-20, iced tea tumbler $20-22. Front row: cordial $20-25, sherbet $15-18, dessert bowl $40-45, juice tumbler $15-18.

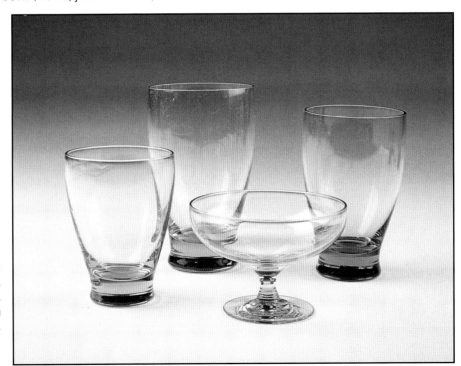

American Modern Coral: juice tumbler $15-18, iced tea tumbler $20-22, sherbet $15-18, luncheon tumbler $18-20.

American Modern stemware: (from left) Crystal cordial $20-25, Crystal wine
$20-25, Seafoam cocktail $20-25, Granite Grey (Smoke) goblet $15-18.

Seafoam glassware.
Goblet $25-30, juice
tumbler $20-25,
cocktail $20-25.

American Modern glassware ordering form.

DISTINGUISHED ADDITIONS

TO THE *Russel Wright*
american modern
COLORED GLASSWARE COLLECTION

american modern*
COLORED GLASSWARE
DESIGNED BY

Russel Wright

american modern
COLORED GLASSWARE
DESIGNED BY

Russel Wright

Hand-blown stemware and glassware of fine bell-tone quality especially designed and colored by Russel Wright . . . to complement famous Russel Wright American Modern Dinnerware, hand-made by Steubenville Pottery.

	Fixed Retail Price EACH	8 PC. SET
Double Old Fashioned	$ .70	$4.80
Pilsner	1.20	8.45
Chilling Bowl	1.85	14.50

Colors: Chartreuse, Granite Gray, Coral, Seafoam and Crystal.

Follow Handy Order Sheet on Reverse Side.

Please check here if you wish additional Glassware___ order blanks for handy future use.

* Reg. U.S. Pat. Off.

---

american modern
COLORED GLASSWARE
DESIGNED BY *Russel Wright*

TUMBLERS

	Fixed Retail Price EACH	8 PC. SET
Ice Tea	70c	$4.80
Luncheon	60c	4.20
Juice	55c	3.60
Dessert dish	60c	4.20

Colors: Chartreuse, Granite Gray, Coral and Seafoam.

STEMWARE

	EACH	8 PC. SET
Goblet	85c	$6.00
Sherbet	85c	6.00
Cocktail	85c	6.00
Wine	85c	6.00
Cordial	85c	6.00

Colors: Chartreuse, Granite Gray, Coral, Seafoam and Crystal.

12-PIECE TUMBLER SET

4 Ice Tea, 4 Luncheon,
4 Juice Tumblers, Set ... $6.60

TEAR HERE AND MAIL

---

american modern
COLORED GLASSWARE
HANDY ORDER SHEET

To order 12-piece Tumbler Set check below:
4 Ice Tea, 4 Luncheon, 4 Juice Tumblers, Set $6.60 (Your choice of one color only)

NO. OF SETS	COLOR	TOTAL

To order 8-Piece Sets or single pieces, check correct column below.

ITEM	COLOR	NO. OF SINGLE SHAPES	NO. OF 8-PIECE SETS	PRICE
Ice Tea				
Luncheon				
Juice				
Dessert Dish				
Goblet				
Sherbet				
Cocktail				
Wine				
Cordial				
	TOTAL AMOUNT	$		

12-piece Tumbler Sets ordered, amount ....
Single shapes and 8-piece Sets ordered, amount ... $ ....
Total Amount _____

NAME _____
ADDRESS _____
CITY _____ ZONE ___ STATE _____

HANDY ORDER SHEET

NEW ADDITIONS TO
american modern
COLORED GLASSWARE
DESIGNED BY *Russel Wright*

To order 8-Piece Sets or single pieces, check correct column below.

ITEM	COLOR	NO. OF SINGLE SHAPES	NO. OF 8-PIECE SETS	PRICE
Double Old Fashioned				
Pilsner				
Chilling Bowl				
	TOTAL AMOUNT	$		

NAME _____
ADDRESS _____
CITY _____ ZONE ___ STATE _____

American Modern Colored Glassware may be ordered from your local franchised dealer.

Original label on American Modern glassware. Adds $5 to value of piece.

Imperial Pinch tumblers in Smoke. Iced tea $25-30, water $22-25, juice $20-22.

Imperial Pinch tumblers in Verde. Juice $25-30, water $30-35, iced tea $30-35.

Ruby tumblers. $100-125 each

Chartreuse pinch tumblers:
Water $22-25, iced tea $25-30,
juice $20-22.

Thin Smoke pinch tumblers:
Water $25-30, iced tea $30-35,
juice $25-30.

Thin pinch tumblers: Chartreuse juice $30-35, Crystal
water $40-45, Pink iced tea $40-50.

Pinch thin tumblers: Aqua ice tea $65-75, Crystal iced tea
$40-45, Purple/Blue water $75-100, Crystal water $40-45.

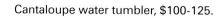
Cantaloupe water tumbler, $100-125.

Imperial Flair tumblers, $100-125 each.

Imperial Twist tumblers: Crystal old fashioned $40-50, Seafoam water $45-50, Crystal water $40-45, Smoke iced tea $45-50.

Twist juice tumblers. Crystal $35-40, Smoke $35-40.

Paden City Snow Glass: water tumbler $225-250, 8" plate $100-125, juice tumbler $200-225, 5" fruit bowl $150-175.

Store advertisement for Eclipse glassware.

Snow Glass pitcher $1500-2000.

Theme Formal glassware. Cordial $200-225, cocktail $125-150, wine $150-175, water $200-225. Theme informal tumbler, $200-225.

Bartlett-Collins' Eclipse tumblers and ice tub. Ice tub, $40-50.

Eclipse tumblers: Yellow zombie $18-20, blue water $15-18, green old fashioned $15-18, straight-sided juice $10-12, blue old fashioned $12-15, blue cordial $12-15, flamingo shot $15-18.

Several different blanks were used for the Eclipse glassware.

Magazine advertisement for Eclipse.

Three eclipse shot glasses, flamingo, green, and blue. $15-18

Original box for Eclipse Zombies. $100-125.

Asterisk/Solar glassware. Iced tea $20-25, water tumbler $20-25, double old fashioned $20-25.

Asterisk/Solar glassware. This represents all the pieces that we have been able to locate. Other sizes may exist. Ice tub, $60-70.

Bibliography

Hennessey, William J. *Russel Wright, American Designer.* Cambridge, MA: MIT Press, 1983.

Kerr, Ann. *The Collectors Encyclopedia of Russel Wright Volume 2.* Paducah, Kentucky: Schroeder Publishing Co., Inc., 1998.

Wright, Russel and Mary. *Guide to Easier Living.* New York: Simon and Schuster, 1950.

It's a stark, profound piece of art, and a visually arresting one. Beautifully and reverentially crafted, known to bring viewers to tears, it has a clear message, and an important story to tell. That combination of straightforwardness, purpose, and fine craftsmanship is Hayes's trademark.

It's one that evolved from his first, early love of creating. Early on in graduate school at Savannah College of Art and Design, Hayes says he was alienated by the self-referential language of art. "I didn't have the vocabulary to talk about my work, to say, this is what it means. I was just interested in making things."

In his second week there, he crocheted a life-size skeleton, taking the time to depict every bone meticulously. "I didn't have any idea what it meant," he says. "I just wanted to make something that was going to be . . . amazing. I wasn't thinking about the concept behind everything. I didn't want the everyday person to have to walk up to text on the side of the wall to understand what the work means. I wanted him to come with their everyday experience to understand what the work means."

When he came upon the idea for *Cash Crop!*, Hayes combined his love of making things with a deep calling to draw attention to the immorality of trading human beings as commodities. "I didn't know the impact that the work was going to make on people," he says. "I just knew that I had something I wanted to make. I stayed in [the studio] days and nights. Sometimes I didn't even eat or sleep. The studio was probably about 15 foot by 15 foot, in the basement of a parking garage. And it took me five months. Day and night."

Hayes has enough upcoming museum shows and commissions for public art and monuments to keep him just as busy for the foreseeable future: the Charlotte-Mecklenburg Police Department, the Mint Museum, downtown Durham, and the North Carolina Museum of Art are all on his calendar.

His goal with these and any future creations, he says, goes back in part to his motivation as a kindergartener: to make people say "wow."

"I want to make a piece of artwork that's going to stop my audience in their tracks from the first sight of it," he says. Once he has their attention, he hopes to create a conversation. "That conversation adds to my concept as a whole," he says. "I don't want to cut anybody off and tell them, this is what I want you to see. No. I want you to come with wherever you're from . . . and I want us to have that conversation."

He'll need to draw on reserves of focus and productivity, something he clearly has in large supply. "I have this mode that I call 'machine mode,' where I'm just in it," he says. "I'm in it, and I'm just making, and I'm not even thinking about anything else, just get this done. I got a job, I got a task that I need to do, and I need to complete." ▪

FACING
Donald Martiny at work in his
Chapel Hill home studio.

DONALD MARTINY

CHAPEL HILL

If color itself could come alive, dance across a wall, and leave its own mark, it might become the art of Donald Martiny. Freed, is what his works look like, colors freed and unbound, let off the hook of representing anything else, finally allowed to be themselves. The gestures that move them are also let loose. Strokes have escaped from the canvas to swirl and leap and run, to expand, to combine with color, to become the art itself.

"I spend a long time mixing colors, trying to get the color just where I want it to be," he says. "I don't really think about paint as paint, or color as color. I don't use it politically or symbolically at all. It's more like pushing sensation around, I'm pushing ecstasy, or I'm pushing tragedy, I'm pushing the whole spectrum of human feeling around." He uses the word "pushing" literally. The viscous polymer that forms his work is something he shoves and moves with his

hands, with his arms, with his various tools, with his whole body.

It takes all of him to express the particular feeling he's chosen for a particular piece. "I can get in touch with it, much like a method actor does, I can kind of fall into this place and really become that, and then I can paint. And I'm in the paint. I mean I'm literally covered in paint."

The large-scale, free-form, floating brushstroke works that result, painting-sculpture hybrids that defy categorization, hang all over the world. There's a monumental installation at One World Trade Center and one at LAX airport. He's exhibited everywhere from Hong Kong to Padua and spent the last several years working seven days a week, crisscrossing the globe for solo shows, major commissions, and art fair exhibitions in Asia, Europe, and the Middle East. "It's a lot, but it's good. There's never, ever any downtime. There's always something to do, or something to figure out."

Some of that's conceptual, some is technical. Martiny points out eight different experiments he's running to test drying times for various oil paints, a tricky medium for him. Most of his work is made with a polymer base he developed to allow for his sculptural technique, to enable his several-inches-thick pieces to dry relatively quickly without shriveling, and to ensure they stand the test of time. He actually ran the material through an accelerator test and found it lasted over 500 (theoretical) years without deterioration.

Martiny's color, of course, is also his own. With a Heilscher ultrasonic machine, Martiny pulverizes various materials into fine powders to create customized, hypersaturated pigments. Once mixed with his polymer, these pigments can become paint that's glossy or matte or transparent to suit Martiny's needs. He can change its viscosity; he can tweak its "rheology," making it pour like honey or clot like cottage cheese.

This technical expertise came from years of experimenting to find a way to make his artistic vision possible. A lifelong student of art and art history, Martiny painted "very realistic" landscapes early on but felt hemmed in by the canvas. "It occurred to me that the rectangle is a portal, or a window, that you're looking through to experience the art in a different place. And for me, it was really important to have a very intimate connection with the viewer. . . . I wanted the art experience to be in front of the portal, not behind the portal. And also, I didn't need a rectangle as a form. That didn't make any sense, really."

It might not make sense for Martiny, but it's important to him that his work honor and refer to work that came before, that it has "a dialogue with the history of art. If art is going to have a lasting presence, it has to have a strong dialogue with the history. So I'm constantly looking back. I'm constantly studying." Every morning, he and his wife, the artist Celia Johnson, study together, mostly art history and philosophy.

The work of second-generation abstract expressionists teed him up to create a medium of his own. "You'll see that they often make a strong gesture, one grand gesture, and then they'll fill in the negative spaces." To Martiny,

That diminished the integrity of the initial gesture, and it also took away from the power of it. So I thought, well, let's get rid of that. So all of a sudden I had to get rid of not only the shape of the rectangle, I needed to get rid of the canvas completely. The whole ground. I had to get rid of the ground. And I didn't know how to do that. So I went through years of trying different materials and trying to figure out how to accomplish that technically, even though I had the concept very clearly in my mind. And after years of fooling around with failed paints, I finally came up with something that works. And it's constantly evolving. ∎

FACING
Alo, by Donald Martiny, 2020.
54 × 40 in. Polymer and dispersed pigment on aluminum.

SABA TAJ

DURHAM

People who inhabit dreamlike worlds without the grounding of floors or horizons are the subject of Saba Taj's large-scale portraits. Some float in space, or within fields of color; others recline on beds of flowers or in seats covered with vines. Their gender or race is often ambiguous, and symbolic images surround them, many of which are Islamic, like the Hand of Fatima, an icon of protection; or honeybees, which can represent industry and feminine power; or the evil eye, which protects against the gaze of others. So do glitter and small jewels like pearls and rhinestones, and mirrors surrounded with the distinctive Shisha embroidery typically used to affix small mirrors to clothing. And while her subjects' bodies and faces are partly rendered in fine detail—an arm, a hand, one half of a beautiful face—other parts blur, becoming wisps of smoke or cloud.

These subjects share an abundant mystery, and they share this too: their gaze is direct. With frank and thoughtful eyes, they look right at you. And so in a subtle but powerful twist, with what Taj describes as "an energetic shift," the viewer of the art becomes the looked-upon.

The questions of who looks and who is seen and where the power lies is at the heart of Taj's work as an artist and as an activist. A self-described queer Muslim artist, the Raleigh-born-and-raised daughter of immigrants from Pakistan-administered Kashmir, Taj has many worlds and identities to navigate.

"It's tough to be different," she says. "And I think a lot of folks realize that. It's a very human way to feel. This notion of belonging is a crucial part of our lives." Taj spends a lot of time thinking about belonging, about what it means, how it is nurtured: "One of those ways is through art," she says, especially when people can "see themselves in (art) in ways that are deep and nuanced and interesting."

It's territory she navigates carefully. Lengthy interviews before she paints her subjects enable her to paint them "fully in their dignity, not being objectified." Or labeled. Taj speaks frequently about liminality, about "breaking open binaries" and painting people in all of their complex individuality.

When she served as executive director at the Carrack, an artist-run exhibit space in Durham, Taj was able to put more art in front of more people that did just that. As a post-MFA fellow at the Center for Documentary Studies at Duke, she used her intimate, admittedly subjective process to "get to a truer outcome" in documenting the people she paints. *Laila in Orchids (Interstitial Lush)*, a portrait of her wife, won the top award from among more than 1,500 submissions in the Raleigh Fine Arts Society's forty-first annual North Carolina Artist's Exhibition in 2020. Nat Trotman, a Guggenheim Museum curator, was juror.

Her work has been the subject of numerous other prestigious solo and group exhibits, and she is in

FACING
Saba Taj in the studio where she worked at the Center for Documentary Studies at Duke University, Durham, in front of her *Laila in Orchids (Interstitial Lush)*.

At the Meeting of the Seas, by
Saba Taj, 2020. 72 × 72 in.
Oil paint and glitter on canvas.
Courtesy of Saba Taj.

demand as a speaker on the subjects of gender stud-ies, the power of representation, and resilience. Taj also works in other media, including sculpture and performance; the collages in her *Monsters* series, rife with Islamic imagery, address apocalypse and rebirth. A series of illustrations titled *Nazar*, which includes figures riddled, sporelike, with concentric circles that represent the evil eye, addresses the be-lief that one can be harmed by the gaze of others.

The ability to raise difficult questions and depict truths through art is one Taj has explored since she was a child. Support from her parents and a broad education, including Raleigh's Ravenscroft School, an undergraduate art education degree from NC Central, and an MFA from UNC–Chapel Hill, enabled her to navigate "a number of different environments that ask for conformity in some pretty intense ways and in ways I could never really deliver."

In her art and through her activism it seems clear that Taj has found her belonging. "The South feels like home to me," she says. "It's everything I've known. Durham in particular—I feel so rooted here, and so surrounded by my people." These are the people of art and also of activism. It's "because of the really import-ant work that happens in the South, the folks who are organizing around . . . how systems are oppressing certain groups of people . . . that makes me feel like I have belonging in a really important way." ∎

STACY LYNN WADDELL

DURHAM

"My work started out being about history, and finding a place where I could insert myself in history, specifically American history," says artist Stacy Lynn Waddell. "And then it became more and more about identity. And now it has come to be about the issues of representation. Who gets to be represented and how? Why is it that representation matters, and who gets to decide that?"

Known nationally for her multimedia work that showcases transformative techniques including branding, gilding, and singeing, Waddell's art makes statements about representation and also about beauty, power, and history, and the ways they are marked and recorded.

In this portrait, Waddell holds an emergency blanket, one of many materials that have fueled her work. Representative of an inexpensive heat-conserving material often given to refugees or "people caught migrating," the material itself is a source of power and fascination: inert while flat, life-giving when manipulated. In various pieces, she has mimicked emergency blankets with gilded, crumpled paper. Shapeshifting, literally and metaphorically, is a central theme.

"The idea of me being seen [in this portrait] with materials is apt," she says. "In the studio, a main inspiration is engaging with the materials first, and then thinking about what they can be." The transformation of two-dimensional things into sculptural forms is a recurring process in her work.

Stacy Lynn Waddell in her Durham studio.

THE TWO OF US CROUCHING DOWN WITH HALOS AS HATS (for M. S.),
by Stacy Lynn Waddell, 1973/2021. 60 × 48 in. Composition gold leaf
on canvas. Photograph by Kunning Huang.

In Waddell's gilded diptych *Battle Royal*, flat sheets of gold leaf covered paper are debossed with the images of two guns pointed at one another in a stand-off. One gun is similar to that used by Harriet Tubman, and the other is a standard-issue Glock. These faintly three-dimensional images require careful study, something Waddell encourages. "You have to move your body around the piece to take it all in. In that way it's sculptural," encouraging a "360-degree experience with the work" both physically and mentally.

Her branded and singed paper works—also faintly three-dimensional, as the act of branding or singeing makes not only a burn but an indentation—are also best appreciated with careful study, she says.

"I'm a slow looker," she says. "I find myself returning to work again and again and again. It's the reason I fell in love with museums as a child . . . like libraries, which I also loved and still do, you can return to that same place in the stacks, and look at those books or through those books. In a museum, I can go to the same works that I love in the permanent collections and in galleries and have a relationship with them."

For the Mint Museum's 2021 exhibition *Silent Streets: Art in the Time of the Pandemic*, Waddell worked with quilter Ginny Robinson to create a series of three flags—one red, one white, and one blue—each dedicated to a Black woman or group of Black women. The red flag, made of heirloom textiles, honors her maternal grandmother and her role building a loving family legacy. Made of vintage Cone Mills denim, the blue flag honors a 1960s-era group of women at Raleigh's Shaw University who marched against Jim Crow laws wearing denim, in solidarity with Black farmers and other laborers.

And the white flag, made of nineteenth- and twentieth-century lace, silk, and linen that had been deaccessioned from the Mint Museum's collection, Waddell dedicated to Harriet Tubman, "our Moses, who first chose freedom for herself then led many out from bondage as a conductor on the Underground Railroad, never losing a passenger while carrying a pistol, singing songs of liberation and avoiding those that would call for her death." Waddell's description continues: "Thirty-four years after the Emancipation Proclamation, and a life of faith and tireless service, she accepted gifts of adoration from Queen Victoria, the granddaughter of Queen Sophia Charlotte, Great Britain's first biracial royal of African and German descent, and namesake of the largest city in North Carolina."

Waddell is a graduate of UNC–Chapel Hill's MFA program. Her art has been exhibited widely, including in the State of the Art 2020 show at Crystal Bridges Museum of American Art; in a Dexter Wimberly-curated show at the Harvey B. Gantt Center for African American Arts + Culture in Charlotte; and at the Prizm Art Fair in Miami during Art Basel, among many other shows. Waddell's work is in the collections of the Gibbes Museum of Art in Charleston, South Carolina, the North Carolina Museum of Art, the Studio Museum in Harlem, and the Pennsylvania Academy of the Fine Arts in Philadelphia, among several other public collections. ▪

DAMIAN STAMER

DURHAM

In his pristine, purpose-built studio, with his paints lined up in rows and his brushes clean and sorted, Damian Stamer paints disintegration. Old barns and abandoned houses, abstracted, exposed, collapsed, and undone. They are filled with broken things. Some seem to have exploded, to be in the process of warp-speed deterioration.

Stamer was a kid on a bike with his twin when he first began exploring places like this. On back roads and fields around his Durham County home, forgotten shacks and moldering tobacco barns leaned toward the land and drew him in, fascinating not only as relics of the past but as ruins in continuing evolution. Rusted tools and warped shelves gave way to stained mattresses and empty liquor bottles; nature made its relentless, long-game effort to reclaim. It has never let him go.

Stamer loads a pallet knife with a glob of grey-blue oil paint and smudges it in the lower right corner of a painting underway. It's close to finished, an abstracted greyscale barn interior. The center is pale and bright, as if you've come inside on a sunny day and your eyes are still adjusting. Around the edges, shapes emerge: a broken pipe, a dented washtub, some sort of grate. The longer you look, colors turn up, too. Turns out there are slashes, garish slashes, of bright orangey-red, and swaths of yellow, and scribbles in many shades of green. Texture, too: wood-grain-patterned slats, grit on the floor, mist in the air, some sort of acid-drop speckles, like dust motes or floaters. It all has the gauzy, open-ended feeling of a memory, of a dream, of a subconscious question: What is home? What do we build? How long does it last?

Stamer stands back to assess the mark he's just made. He goes back, scrapes some off, smears it in the opposite corner.

"I try to keep surprising myself, in a way. Doing unexpected things. Even messing things up." He gestures to a section of the panel where he's now added several marks. "There's stuff about what I just laid down, some things I don't love right now, but then you let it dry, scrape it down, and then there's that remnant coming through. It can be very gorgeous." He looks back again, studies it some more. "I try not to get too attached to any part. To not make anything too precious."

Working on panel allows him to treat it that way, to work the surface hard, to erode and scratch away and then build back up. The studio itself also frees him. Built to his specifications and designed with his father, a structural engineer, it has enormous walls—Stamer prefers painting on them as opposed to on easels, and is able to hang his work on them, even the largest pieces, the ones that are six feet tall and almost eight feet wide. "I see them as museum pieces, or institutional pieces . . . they're on a scale that could really fill up a wall."

They are, in fact, on the walls of museums and institutions around the world. Crystal Bridges Museum placed his work front and center in its *State of the Art 2020* show; he has had solo exhibitions in Tokyo, New York, Budapest, and Charleston among other places in the last few years, and is in several prestigious public and private collections.

A proud graduate of the UNC School of the Arts high school with an MFA from UNC–Chapel Hill, he considers Anselm Kiefer an inspiration and Beverly McIver a mentor and has never forgotten where he came from, or what first inspired him all those years ago, a kid getting lost in the landscape. Because even

as he paints decay, Stamer's subject is also wonder. In every painting of falling-down walls, of mouse-gnawed floorboards, and forgotten furniture, the details betray an ardent fascination. And also hope. Light (there is always a source of light, an exit, or a portal, and sometimes, as in *St. Mary's Rd. 8*, one with an unmistakably celestial aura) is a recurring beacon, a relief, a magnet.

"Creatively," he says, "it really goes back and forth between the plan of creating a space, and then kind of blowing that up, and putting it back together again. It's like an intuitive dance. . . . You try to think and not think at the same time." ∎

ABOVE
St. Mary's Rd. 8, by Damian Stamer, 2018–20. 72 × 95 in. Oil on panel. Photograph by Christopher Ciccone.

FACING
Chieko Murasugi with several of her works in her Chapel Hill home studio.

CHIEKO MURASUGI

CHAPEL HILL

Abstract painter Chieko Murasugi has navigated conflicting perspectives all her life. She is a PhD in visual science who works as an artist; she is the Tokyo-born daughter of Japanese immigrants who was raised in Toronto and lives in the United States; she is a former impressionist painter who now uses visual illusion to anchor her geometric art.

"I want to make the elusive, disparate, confusing, multifaceted nature of the world absolutely clear. I want to be clear in my view that the world is unclear."

Illusions underpin this message; her interest in them is one of the few things that has remained constant in her life. As a scientist, Murasugi studied visual perception because she was fascinated by mysteries like 3D illustrations that seem to flip, the ghosts of afterimages, and the way the perception of a color changes depending on the colors that sit beside it. Now, as an artist, she uses phenomena like these to tweak a viewer's perception, to make a picture plane shift before their eyes, to turn it from

one thing into another. She populates these paintings with crisp, unambiguous, flat-colored shapes. "I have clarity and I have ambiguity at the same time," she says. "And that's really at the crux of my art. It's the ambiguity, the clarity, the dichotomy."

Her art creates it, and she's long lived it. Murasugi grew up in a "very white" Canadian suburb, "very clearly a minority." As a child, her father, a descendant of 1600s-era Samurais, showed her maps of Japan's former reach across Asia, and told her "Americans took it away." He told her about how American forces firebombed downtown Tokyo, and how he and her mother barely escaped with their lives.

But these were not facts she'd been taught in school, or heard anywhere else. "I had taken world history, and I had not heard anything about the firebombings of Japan," she says. "And so everywhere I went, I was presented with diverging, often conflicting, but very disparate narratives. Who am I supposed to believe?" When she was studying for her PhD in visual science at York University in Canada, she recalls, her professors proudly touted the department's prominence in the field. Then she went to Stanford to do her postdoctoral work in neurobiology, and nobody had heard of her colleagues at York University. "And again, I had to shift my perspective." Fueling those shifts was an overwhelming curiosity, "always wanting to know why. Why, why, why. Curiosity has been the driving force of my life."

Years later, when Murasugi left her accomplished academic career and the world of science for art (she had always drawn and painted, and studied art in college as well as science), her viewpoint shifted again. In a deeply rooted way, she was coming home. Because, even at the height of her successful scientific career, Murasugi believed that she didn't truly belong. She thought she wasn't quantitative, logical, or analytical enough, that "there was something that was missing in the way that I was thinking." With art, the opposite was the case: "I knew I could do it."

This innate conviction took her back to school, to UNC-Chapel Hill for an MFA, where she met fellow artists she respected and joined with to cofound and cocurate an artist-run exhibit space called Basement.

The art she makes now assumes nothing of a viewer's point of view. It has been exhibited in museums in San Francisco, New York, and across the South and is in the collections of the City of Raleigh and Duke University.

Its abstraction welcomes any interpretation at all; its subtle illusory elements gently subvert them. "People have said to me over the years: Your work is so beautiful. And I think, well, I hope it doesn't stop there. But if they say it's so beautiful—Oh! And then it flips! I think, OK, good. As long as they see that there were two ways of looking at it." ▪

WILLIAM PAUL THOMAS

DURHAM

What would it change if the adversity people suffer silently was plainly visible to the outside world? Would we treat one another differently if a person's trauma could be seen on their face?

These are among the questions William Paul Thomas poses with his moving portraits. He calls the series *Cyanosis*, referring to the bluish cast that can color the skin when blood is starved of oxygen. The hue also serves to highlight the natural color of his subjects' skin. "I was interested in finding a different way to express my own relationship to race," he says, one that didn't rely on what he considers negative "tropes."

"I thought if I altered the skin color, then that would be something you would have to talk about: their skin color, if nothing else, being changed. And what that might signify."

As a Black artist, he says, "No matter what you make, it has the capacity to be framed or centered on your identity, but you still have a choice to decide

what the content is." In each of his nuanced portraits, the humanity of his subjects is central. He hopes viewers will consider what's beyond the canvas: "A person's emotional expression, your inference about their psychological state, the setting that they're in, their status in life, their vocation . . ."

He names each of these works for a woman who loves the man depicted. "What does it mean," he asks, "if I am celebrating these men, and asking us to consider that they are loved by a woman, or a girl, or a daughter, or a mother. Does that change the way we see their value?"

Viewers inevitably bring their own perspectives, which he welcomes. Some, Thomas says, see his paintings as symbols of empowerment; see the blue, for example, as the color of royalty, of a team, or even of a superhero mask. "There are so many ways to interpret color."

Another color prominent in Thomas's work is hot pink. It's the shade he painted the cinder block brick he uses in a series of video works and photographs. It symbolizes the color his mother painted the cinder block walls of the Chicago apartment they lived in when he was a child. It evokes his origins, his early influences, and his gratitude for a mother who made the best of her circumstances.

Thomas credits both his mother and his grandmother for encouraging him to draw as a child, for nurturing the talent that had him thinking of himself as an artist from a very early age, that took him to the University of Wisconsin to major in art.

North Carolina became home when he came to Chapel Hill for his MFA, and the state has been good to him, he says. His work has been widely exhibited, he has taught art at Duke and at Guilford College in Greensboro, held several prestigious residencies, and curated group shows at galleries, including *Opulence, Decadence* at Lump Gallery in Raleigh. ∎

THOMAS SAYRE

RALEIGH

Thomas Sayre's sculptures serve as beacons and focal points across North Carolina and around the world. His three-ring *Gyre* has become an icon and symbol of Raleigh's North Carolina Museum of Art. His massive spheres and series of roomlike sculptures stretch 400 yards down a central quad at the University of Colorado in Denver. On Thailand's island of Phuket, Sayre's conical tower surveys the Andaman Sea. These works—cast in and of the earth, or made of metal or fiberglass—are as varied as they are numerous.

Some are light and playful, like Tampa, Florida's *Ripple*, which invites pedestrians to the waterfront with stainless steel squiggles. Some are cool and clever, like the thirty giant polished spheres of *Curveball* that represent the path of a sinking fast pitch and a home run at Washington, DC's Nationals Stadium. Many others, like the five curving pillars of *Oberlin Rising* that honor a historic Raleigh freedmen's community, are tributes.

Each of them is also a celebration: of the earth and of humankind, and of how they meet, intersect, and diverge. In that way, they also reflect the artist. The great-grandson of US president Woodrow Wilson and onetime Morehead Scholar at UNC–Chapel Hill is nothing if not cerebral, taking care with each of his works to reflect and honor their place, purpose, and story. He is also an engineer, able to take these abstract ideas and make them massively, physically real.

Thomas Sayre with a recently completed thirty-foot-high earthcast sculpture at the corner of Cary Parkway and Evans Road in Cary, 2021.

When asked to describe how he made a pagoda out of stacked earthcast discs for a Raleigh collector, for instance—Sayre begins with the process, the placement of rebar, the casting of concrete, the role of traction and hand tooling and plate welding, even the awkward angle required of the crane to lift and place each disc. The practical puzzle of it all is clearly satisfying to solve. But it's when Sayre gets to the meaning behind the work that he comes alive. He talks about the purpose of a pagoda as a marker for a place where prayer can happen, of the similarity between the shape of a pagoda and that of a ladder, and of Jacob's ladder, on which angels ascended and descended, and of the last sermon his own father gave about a dream he'd had in which his own mother was one of those angels (Francis Sayre Jr. served as the dean of Washington National Cathedral for twenty-seven years), and about heaven and earth, and the connection between the two.

"For me, it's about living on this earth informed by the God above," Sayre says. "And there are intermediaries—angels—and there are devices—pagodas—that help with this connection."

These are not new themes for Sayre. He grew up not only in the heart of a national house of prayer and the Episcopal Church but also alongside a Buddhist, a Thai boy, the nephew of that country's king, who lived with the Sayre family for eighteen years.

On the day of the Raleigh pagoda's excavation, and again on the day of its installation, Sayre bows to the earth to pray with Buddhist Van Nolintha, who commissioned the work. He prays "that the Buddha,

Thomas Sayre excavating an earthcast disk, part of a stacked pagoda sculpture for a Raleigh collector.

and God, and Yahweh, and Mohammad would smile on this effort that was for the good of the world. And for the energy to do it. And to bring the sacred in."

To understand how Sayre works, it's important to witness these two realms, and how they intersect. Literally and metaphorically, the spaces in which he works represent two sides of his brain: one ruminative, allegorical, creative; the other practical, tactical, physical.

The first of these is Sayre's studio, until recently situated in a series of large open spaces inside a former industrial building in Raleigh's Warehouse District. (He and his late business partner, architect Steve Schuster, were among the earliest residents of this neighborhood.) The studio is where he thinks, where he paints, where he researches and experiments, where he makes the maquettes—or sculptural models—that precede his monumental works.

The second is the field, where he uses heavy machinery to dig sculptural forms in the earth, where he fills them with rebar and cement and earth, where he later digs up hardened shapes, lifts them with a crew and a crane, and situates and embeds them where they belong.

The point where the earth ends and man-made concrete begins, he says, fascinates him.

His wife, Jed, jokes that Sayre must have an especially large corpus callosum, or connective tissue between the left and right sides of his brain, and it probably helps that the artist inhabits both of these sides as physical spaces, worlds that require very different skills. Also that he allows each to inform the other. Sayre's engineering brain is never absent as he dreams up sculptural forms; his artistic brain allows serendipity and insight to inform even the real-time, heavy-machinery-intense completion of his work.

The difference between the shapes he plans and the ones he gets, he'll tell you, is where the magic lies. Along the way, there's a lot that can go wrong, and sometimes does.

That's less often true with his paintings, in which paint is seldom present, and technique is often sculptural. Using browny-black tar as a medium, Sayre smears and scrapes and gouges, creating fields of cotton bolls in one series. In another, flung molten metal creates thickets of trees. The smoke of a welding torch creates other paintings filled with wispy-heavy, cloudlike shapes. In others, the holes and dents that bullets leave in metal form the stars of a flag or the surface of a cross.

Sayre's work can be found in public places across the country and internationally. He has exhibited his work in numerous galleries and museums, and is the recipient of a National Endowment of the Arts Fellowship. He was awarded an honorary doctorate of fine arts from NC State University and the North Carolina Award, the state's highest civilian honor. ∎

BEVERLY McIVER

Beverly McIver paints to make sense of the world and her life, the people she loves and the things they go through. Her ability to capture humanity in the process—to communicate hard, complicated, and joyful truths—has made her one of the most revered artists painting in America today, named among the Top Ten in Painting by *Art News*.

Portraits of her father she made until his passing at the age of ninety-five, of her mentally disabled sister Renee, and of herself are among McIver's best-known works. Together they examine race and dignity, worth and purpose, persona and authenticity, duty and love.

In 2020, the isolation of COVID brought about a period of introspection and productivity for McIver. Her self-portraits began to take on darker aspects. In many, her face is covered or obscured by slatted shadows, scarves, or tangles of rope. Her eyes are often closed.

"I think the rope and scarf were about being claustrophobic," she says, "about being trapped in this life. And realizing that I am not doing enough. I am not making enough of a difference in the world."

She'd had a taste of making a difference when the People for the American Way commissioned her (and other major artists like Shepard Fairey and Carrie Mae Weems) to create a painting on the theme of "Enough of Trump" in advance of the 2020 election. The group put her work on giant billboards in swing states. "I don't think of my work as being political, but I enjoyed seeing the power of the billboards," she says.

A different form of power is behind another plan to make a difference: the creation of an artist's residency for women and people of color on her Chapel Hill property, one that pays a stipend. Tod Williams and Billie Tsien, the architects of the Obama Presidential Library, have offered to design it for her without charge.

McIver has been inspired to create the nonprofit residency by her own experiences. "I've done some of my best work at residencies," she says, "but I get so worked up and anxious. I know I'm going to be the only Black person. I know they're going to eat food I traditionally don't eat. You have to be so flexible, so open, and extend yourself in a way—it becomes a challenge just to show up."

That was true even during the year she lived and worked in Rome as a recipient of the American Academy's prestigious Rome Prize in 2017. Despite its challenges, McIver found the opportunity remarkable. With swaths of time to paint and no household or familial responsibilities to tend, she "went inside," she says. "To identify who I was without Renee, without my dad standing in front of me, to figure out who I am and what that person looks like." The experience served as a kind of palate cleanser: "The biggest thing I learned in Rome is that if you're willing to be open," she says, "it's amazing what will come your way. The scary part is just being open to it."

The idea that McIver was ever scared of anything is hard to imagine, as fearlessness has long shaped her life, beginning with her childhood in a Greensboro

FACING
Beverly McIver with several of her works in her studio at Duke University, Durham.

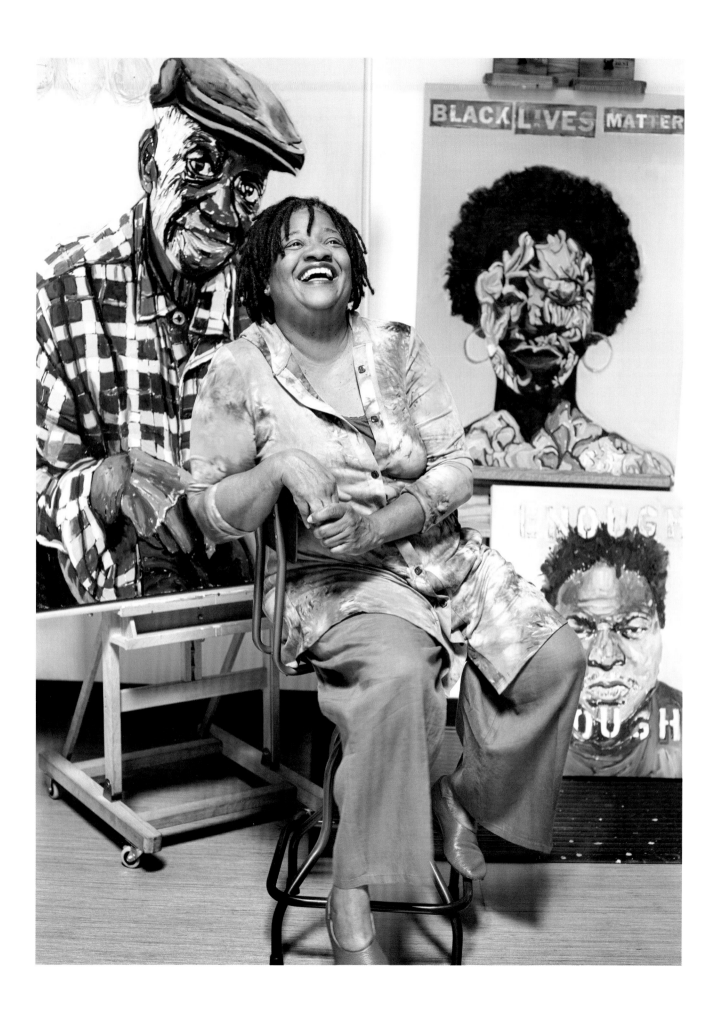

housing project as the daughter of a single mother who worked as a maid and a father she didn't meet until she was sixteen.

McIver only started painting as an undergraduate at NC Central University as a lark. Despite encouragement from her professors, she was wary of pursuing art as a career, worried she'd never be able to support herself. But once she dove in, accolades quickly followed. McIver received a Guggenheim Fellowship, a Radcliffe Fellowship, and many other awards.

At every stage of her career, truth, she says, has always been her aim: "I'm trying to do things that bring me closer to my authentic self. I think that's what people see."

A career survey of her work opened at the Scottsdale Museum of Contemporary Art in 2022 before traveling to SECCA in Winston-Salem. McIver's art can be found in the collections of the National Portrait Gallery at the Smithsonian, the North Carolina Museum of Art, the Weatherspoon Art Museum, the Baltimore Museum of Art, the NCCU Art Museum, the Asheville Museum of Art, the Crocker Art Museum, the Nelson Fine Arts Center Art Museum at Arizona State University, the Nasher Museum of Art at Duke University, the Cameron Art Museum, and the Mint Museum, as well as significant corporate and private collections. McIver is currently the Ebenshade Professor of the Practice in Studio Arts at Duke University. ∎

FACING
Grief, by Beverly McIver, 2022. 30 × 40 in.
Oil on canvas. Courtesy of the artist and
Craven Allen Gallery.

PATRICK DOUGHERTY

CHAPEL HILL

If a potter could live inside a pot, or a painter could dwell within a painting, they might feel almost as at home as sculptor Patrick Dougherty clearly does. The stick sculpture artist lives in a house in the woods that he made from the logs he gathered there. It stands behind a stick fence, beyond a herringboned wooden outbuilding, down a long gravel driveway, and tucked into twenty rural Orange County acres.

The result, like Dougherty's art, is a self-contained environment at one with nature: part of it, informed by it, and also otherworldly. Woven, spun, braided, and twirled, his massive, cocoon-like works of art look like nests shot out of a hurricane. In places that dot the globe—from Belgrade to Sewanee, Charleston to Dublin—they are meant to be entered and explored, experienced and touched. Over the last thirty-plus years, he has built more than 300 of these giant works, ten of them a year, three weeks at a time, and always with a cadre of local volunteers.

The Oklahoma native likens the process of sculpting with sticks to "drawing with lines in the air." The technique is to "concentrate on using the tapers to your advantage," he says. "What happens is you get an implied motion. And so these things have a quality of motion to them, and not by accident, but by design. You try to make these luxurious surfaces that have depth to them, but also an implied way of moving."

There is, undeniably, an alive quality to his art, a sense that one of his peaky huts might give you a wink, or scamper off when you're not looking. It likely has something to do with that movement he's able to contain within them, but it might also reflect their whimsy, or the many hands that helped, or the fact that they are, in fact, alive, have a life, one that will end, will rot and topple, just like all of ours.

That temporality is part of what has kept Dougherty out of what he calls "the normal art system." Galleries "are trying to make money and they want to sell something," he points out, usually something with lasting value. What Dougherty offers is fleeting. "There's an honesty to it," he says, "because it elucidates the most important part of making art and looking at art, and that is how it makes you feel. The intensity of the moment that you view it. And this work tends to capitalize on that. You see the reaction in people. They can't buy it or sell it, they can't collect it."

But they can experience its creation, interact with it from beginning to end, the way they can't with almost any other type of visual art, and even if they aren't part of the making, they can step inside and experience it once it's done. "I don't have any fences up around my work," he says. "People have access to the process during the entire [construction]. So the person who's calling the police on the first day about the material being thrown on the ground is asking you to dinner on the last day." In between, they've witnessed, and maybe helped, turn a pile of sticks into a work of art. They've come to care about it, worry about it, fuss over it, take pride in it.

"The magic of it is conjured by me, but it seems beguilingly simple, because I'm having different

FACING
Patrick Dougherty at work, assembling
Common Ground at Davidson College,
Davidson, NC, 2020.

people work on different aspects of it; we're all working fruitfully as a group. Oftentimes, my volunteers say: 'I'm not even sure we needed you.'" He laughs. "That's an illusion they carry because they feel so good about how they worked. And that goodwill translates right into the community at large."

Dougherty, who is married to Linda Dougherty, chief curator and curator of contemporary art at the North Carolina Museum of Art, came into the art world on his own terms, and relatively late. The UNC–Chapel Hill graduate earned an undergraduate degree in English and a master's in hospital and health administration before heading back to UNC at thirty-six to study art. By the early '80s, he was combining his love of nature with his knowledge of sculpture and carpentry to create works made of saplings. From the beginning, he's known he wanted to make art that appeals to "the fine art painter and the house painter."

The first big piece he made as a student, a "mummified-looking thing" made out of "really fine sticks" gathered in his backyard, won a statewide award, got him a show at SECCA in Winston-Salem, and led to residencies, grants, and more awards. Slowly but surely, he was working all over the East Coast. He decided to step onto a wider stage after a visiting professor from Hunter College, the ceramic artist Susan Peterson, told him that it was "just as easy to be a national artist as it is to be a local artist," and that the only difference was "you have to be willing to be in the nation."

"And so," he says, "I've spent the last thirty years being in the nation. . . . And no matter where I go, whether it would be a rural community or an urban community, what I see is that people are intensely interested in a great visual experience. . . . If they see something that stirs them, that speaks to different aspects of the human condition, they're there. They want it, they want to see it, they want to experience it." ∎

The completed *Common Ground* at Davidson College, Davidson, NC, 2020. 60 × 30 × 18 ft. Mixed hardwoods. Photograph courtesy of Davidson College and David Ramsey.

IVANA MILOJEVIC BECK

When a person moves from a native country to live in a foreign one, they seldom leave the first entirely behind. More often, immigrants inhabit both places, toggling between them, with body, mind, spirit, and culture sometimes in one place, sometimes the other, and sometimes in a third place of their own devising.

Ivana Milojevic Beck, who left her native Serbia as a teenager and now lives in Raleigh with her American husband and young daughter, has turned her bifurcated heart and life into art.

Using the unlikely media of bricks and wax, Milojevic Beck melts, pours, molds, chisels, and forges sculpture that represents her immigrant's duality and commands curiosity. With translucent, delicate bodies and sturdy, structural feet, her work is beautiful but confounding. Art made of wax? Art made of bricks? Art made of bricks and wax? This unlikely combination makes perfect sense in its realization, and perfect sense to its maker. "When you see something in front of yourself that matches how you feel, it's a breakthrough. It's very magical."

Wax in her hands is symbolic of the vulnerable and adaptable body; brick represents durability, place, and strength, "the groundwork" of her life. If one brick is in Serbia, and one is in America, in between is a fluid body, one that can withstand high temperatures, adapt to a mold, melt back again, remold into something new. It is soft and organic and difficult to define. When she made the decision to include some structural support within the wax segments of her work, it was a long-considered, difficult one. She knew the work needed the infrastructure so it could last, but she resisted its symbolism. Then she reconsidered: maybe the addition of cables within the wax was symbolic of something real and important: her own evolution into a person who understands the need for strength within fluidity. "It was a natural progression."

The whole process is organic for Beck. When she pours her melted wax, she lets it set however it chooses, "not trying to force the material to do something that naturally it cannot do." It's important to her that her materials are in all ways natural—wax and brick both products of the earth—and that they are distinctly separate as well as combined in her work (she stirs brick dust into the melted wax in order to strengthen it and create its fleshy color. Making holes in the bricks to create that dust "was the first time I saw the brick vulnerable," she says). Some pieces she sets in molds she makes out of galvanized steel, some in holes in the ground.

When Beck was a child in Serbia, living "a spartan existence" and spending a lot of time at home alone, she had to entertain herself. She recalls looking at herself in her grandmother's mirror as a way to connect with a human face. She didn't know what sculpture was, didn't know that being an artist was

FACING
Ivana Milojevic Beck at her
Raleigh home and studio.

something a person could do. Coming to the United States as an au pair opened up a world she didn't know existed. She went on to earn an undergraduate degree and an MFA from UNC Greensboro, and become a studio artist at Artspace in Raleigh. Her work has since been in several prestigious group shows, and won the International Sculpture Center's top student award in 2016.

Today Milojevic Beck is doing a lot of drawing and considering new ways her work can evolve. On her worktable is the first in a series of horseshoe-shaped forms she intends to stack, one on top of the other, several of them in a tower. She gestures with her hands: "I want to see them on top of each other like a column," she says. "I want to see them my height." ∎

Untitled IV, by Ivana Milojevic Beck, 2016. 22 × 16 × 8 in. Brick, wax, and wire. Courtesy of Ivana Milojevic Beck.

JOHN BEERMAN

HILLSBOROUGH

Before John Beerman paints a landscape, he studies the place that's caught his eye and he picks a particular day and time. Maybe it's a low-lit evening in fall, or maybe it's a morning hour that only exists over a span of days in spring, when the angle and energy of the sun provides a certain glow. And then he goes there, day after day, at that appointed hour, to capture that place and that time, building his painting bit by bit until the moment is over, the hour has passed, the shape of light has changed, that bit of season is gone.

To accompany him on one of these plein air excursions is to realize that Beerman doesn't just look like Monet at Giverny, with his straw hat, his wooden easel, his linen shirt and leather shoes, he *looks* like him, looks out through his own eyes at the natural world with the same kind of reverence, looks at it as if it had a soul, a character, and moods, and nuanced beauty, and he learns it, out of a deep respect, and only then does he paint what only he can see.

"I have always found the natural world a gateway to the greater mysteries and meanings of life," Beerman has said. "I've been back here for ten years, in North Carolina, after thirty, forty years up north. And my appreciation and love of the North Carolina landscape continues to grow. I feel we are so fortunate to be here, in this landscape." At a time when the world faces so many problems, he says, "It's important to see the beauty in this world. It is a healing source."

John Beerman at work on *Chatwood Field, Early Morning* at Chatwood in Hillsborough.

When he arrives at his chosen spot—on this spring morning, a field at Chatwood, the beautiful Hillsborough estate owned at the time by his close friend, the author Frances Mayes—he does it well in advance of his chosen hour, because it takes some time to set up his easel with the idiosyncratic system of clamps and slats he's devised to hold the boards in place that will serve as a perch for his canvas and for the egg tempera paint he's made at home out of pigment and egg yolk and keeps in an airtight jar.

"I've always felt a little bit apart from the trend," he says. "I love history. And one also needs to be in the world of this moment, I understand that. I'm inspired by other artists all the time, old ones, and contemporary ones . . . Piero della Francesca. He's part of my community. Beverly McIver, she's part of my community. One of the things I love about my job is that I get to have that conversation with these folks in my studio, and that feeds me [and the work]." Beerman's work keeps company with some of "these folks" and other greats in the permanent collections of some of the nation's most prestigious museums as well, including at the Metropolitan Museum of Art, the North Carolina Museum of Art, the

Chatwood Field, Early Morning, by John Beerman, 2020. 9 × 12 in. Egg tempera on linen. Photograph by Sara Hecker.

Whitney Museum of American Art, in addition to governor's mansions in New York and North Carolina and countless important private collections.

The paintings that have made his name, celebrated landscapes of the Hudson River, early in his career (he is a direct descendant of Henry Hudson, something he learned only after twenty-five years painting the river), and of North Carolina in later years, and of Tuscany, where he spends stretches of time, share a sense of the sublime, a hyperreal unreality, a fascination with shape and volume, space and light, a restrained emphasis on color, and an abiding spirituality.

Chatwood Field, Early Morning
in progress, en plein air,
at the Chatwood estate in
Hillsborough.

"Edward Hopper said all he ever wanted to do was paint the sunlight on the side of a house," Beerman says. "And I so concur with that. It's as much about the light as it is about the subject." A recent painting of the lighthouse at Nag's Head includes only a looming fragment of that famous black-and-white tower, but it's the glow of coastal sun Beerman has depicted on its surface that makes it unmistakably what it is, where it is.

"With some paintings, I know what I want, and I try to achieve that. And other paintings start speaking back to me." He's talking about another fairly recent painting, of the wide rolling ocean and a fisherman on a pier. As he painted it, childhood memories of Pawleys Island, South Carolina, came into play: "In this old rowboat, we'd go over the waves. And in doing this painting, that came in . . . ahh, maybe that's where I am. Sometimes it bubbles up from memories that are right below the conscious."

Whatever he's painting, Beerman says he's always trying to evolve. "One hopes you're getting closer to what is your core thing, right? And I don't want to get too abstract about it, but to me, that's an artist's job, to find their voice. And even at this ripe old age, 61, I'm still in search of that. And at this time in my life, I feel more free to express what I want to express, and how I want to express it. I don't feel too constrained." ■

CELIA JOHNSON

CHAPEL HILL

The self-contained shapes and colors that move across Celia Johnson's birch panel paintings seem to speak to one another, to react, to bounce, to move aside or collide on purpose. Sometimes they leave a trail as they go. Sometimes they tell a story.

Like a poet with an arsenal of words, Johnson riffs with a "core vocabulary" of shapes. "I've always been attracted to definite shapes. I took watercolor. I took figure drawing. I did all the academic preparation. But from my childhood, I was always codifying things of different colors and different shapes." She

sorted rocks, marbles, and pieces of bark; she found that Colorforms, those plastic, primary-colored circles, squares, and triangles that kids can stick and restick into endless configurations "made a vivid impression."

Much later, Johnson became inspired by Constructivism, the Russian theory that believed art should literally be "constructed" out of component parts and should reflect and live within the modern industrial world. She also studied the work of the Bauhaus, the early twentieth-century modernist German art school

even oblique, but those shapes all mean something important to her. She uses them with a "collage sensibility," a practice that feels innate. Back when she was a graphic designer at Condé Nast, laying out pages for *House Beautiful* in the pre-digital era, she used a similar process to put together spreads.

Her material these days includes special formulations of gesso and acrylic paint made by Golden, the company that pioneered acrylic paint for abstract expressionists in the 1950s and provided Johnson with one of the many prestigious residencies she's won in recent years. She's also been exhibited widely. A group show at her gallery in New York, Kathryn Markel Fine Arts, was one of three that showcased her work in the mostly COVID-barren art world of 2021.

This recent work showcases the careful precision that has long focused Johnson's creations. "I'm taking these chaotic things and I'm putting them in order," she says. "I know there are many painters who take the blank canvas and throw themselves at it without a preconceived idea... but I am someone who is making a puzzle, solving it as I get through it, and finding my way out."

that fused design, craft, and fine art with function (several of whose teachers and students would go on to found North Carolina's own Black Mountain College). But it was when she spent a decade working and studying in Germany that Johnson came upon a source of inspiration that continues to inform her work today. It was heraldry, the system that underlies the creation of coats of arms, flags, and armor. She was immediately drawn to its components and its order, its symbolism and classifications.

At home today, deep in a rural corner of Chapel Hill where she lives with her husband, Donald Martiny, Johnson creates a heraldry of her own. It's subtle, Lately, she's experimenting with taking the shapes from the surface of her paintings off of it entirely and turning them into independent pieces that can stand alone or form part of a grouping. Birch panels cut to her specifications in irregular shapes hang on her studio wall to "orbit," so she can "let them loose and let them fly around." It can't be long before they come in to land. "I absolutely know that there's a transition from chaos to order" in her work, she says. "That's a bedrock thing for me." ∎

FACING
Celia Johnson at work in her Chapel Hill home studio.

ABOVE
Comhrá, by Celia Johnson, 2020.
24 × 21 in. Acrylic on birch panel.
Photograph by Celia Johnson.

MAYA FREELON

DURHAM

Maya Freelon's tissue paper sculptures are abstract, a confluence of kaleidoscopic color and organic shape. They move with a breeze, the passing of a person, the opening of a door. They make powerful, lasting statements with impermanent, inexpensive materials. Most of all, they are inquisitive. *What is art?* they ask. *What's it made of? Who gets to make it? Who decides?*

The work is about "challenging norms—social norms, economic norms, and art norms—by turning tissue paper into a fine work of art," says Freelon. "It's about the fragility of life, and transformation, and the ability to see beauty in a lot of different things."

Often made in collaboration with groups of people, her work celebrates "the communal aspect . . . the ancestral heritage, the connection to quilt-making in my family and the African American tradition of making a way out of no way." Metaphorically and literally, Freelon's work is a manifestation of its maker: beautiful and forthright, vulnerable but unflinching; lithe, elegant, and defiantly individual.

At Miami Art Week in 2019, she was named one of five young artists to watch. She installed massive, wafting tissue paper stalactites at the Smithsonian Arts and Industries Building in Washington, DC, in 2018. She's lived and worked in Madagascar, Eswatini, and Italy as part of the US State Department's Art in Embassies program. She's collaborated with Google and Cadillac, and her work is in the collections of the Smithsonian National Museum of African American History and Culture, the University of Maryland, and UNC–Chapel Hill, among others.

Freelon's talent and expressive ability were apparent early on, and she comes by both naturally as the daughter of two renowned artists and the great-granddaughter of another. Her mother, the jazz singer Nnenna Freelon, is a six-time Grammy Award nominee. Her father was revered architect Phil Freelon, the architect of record of the National Museum of African American History and Culture on the Mall in Washington, DC. His own grandfather was Allan Freelon, a noted impressionist painter whose work was celebrated during the Harlem Renaissance. Her namesake and godmother was the poet Maya Angelou ("Auntie Maya"), a close friend of "Queen Mother" Frances Pierce, Freelon's beloved grandmother. Angelou once described Freelon's work, which she bought for her own collection, as "visualizing the truth about the vulnerability and power of the human being."

When Freelon was a graduate student at the School of the Museum of Fine Arts in Boston, living with her grandmother Pierce, she came upon a stack of multicolored tissue paper in the basement of the house. The paper had most likely been in the same spot for fifty years. Drips from a leaky pipe had mottled the stack over time, moving the color from piece to piece, turning the sheets into gossamer rainbows. Freelon was transfixed, and soon consumed with turning the water-stained tissue paper into art, and using water herself to mark and alter tissue paper, intent on "making something out of nothing." That discovery, born out of her connection to her family, became her signature medium.

Making something out of nothing is part of the inspiration. "I think of a quote from my grandmother, which is that we come from a family of sharecroppers who never got their fair share," she says. Grandmother Pierce's grandchildren and "every Black person making the world a better place" were "our ancestors' wildest dreams," she also said. Freelon considers: "To have survived what it took to get here, and then slavery, and then segregation and racism—we're living within it, and we're still existing, and now we have a chance to thrive."

Personally, Freelon says she's more than thriving. "I've never felt prouder, or better or more grateful that I took the leap, that all of my focus goes to making art and sharing it with the world. . . . I feel like I'm just getting started." ∎

Maya Freelon stands before a portion of *Greater Than or Equal To*, her solo exhibition at Raleigh's Contemporary Art Museum in 2020.

CHAPTER 6

EASTERN NORTH CAROLINA

School's out for summer, but three young high school students are walking the empty hallways of their old Kinston middle school. They're back because they're proud of the art they made in these halls and they're proud of the people they became in the process.

"I painted the girl with the Afro," says Madysen Hawkins, pointing out a larger-than-life figure within a fifty-foot mural. "We are looked down on as being women, and also being Black, and I wanted the little girls here to know that they are somebody that can be heard."

She helped create the mural at Rochelle Middle School in 2018 with fellow students, including K'ala Green and Ja'maya Outlaw, part of a project led by nationally renowned muralist Catherine Hart under the auspices of the smART Kinston organization. The project made her believe in her own creativity, says Green, who plans to become a veterinarian. It also made her proud of her school, where 99 percent

of students are eligible for free lunch. "People think that Rochelle is a bad school, and this showed that we were much more than that."

Founded by Kinston entrepreneur, civic leader, philanthropist, and arts advocate Stephen Hill and administered in conjunction with the North Carolina Arts Council, smART Kinston not only brings arts education to public schoolchildren like these girls, it has used art to breathe new life into the city's once-fading downtown. With Hill's funding, smART Kinston has spearheaded the creation of a twelve-block Arts & Cultural District that includes fifty-four rehabilitated, rainbow-painted, picket-fenced former mill homes, and recruited artists to live in them. It has forged a residency program with Penland School of Craft, commissioned murals and public art throughout downtown, founded an art gallery, and brought art education to the community at large.

"He is a visionary," says Rochelle Middle School principal Felicia Solomon. "He is able to stand where there is nothing, and see something. He is able to see beyond what many of us see." Painting the mural at Rochelle made a huge impact on the kids who made it, she says, but it also materially changed the school in lasting ways. "I moved from believing in the power of art to make a difference to actually knowing that power."

Hill himself first understood art's ability to foster change when he took a trip years ago with the North Carolina Arts Council (an organization he has gone on to serve for many years as board chair). The group traveled to Blannahassett Island, a ten-acre refuge in the middle of the French Broad River in the Blue Ridge Mountains, just a bridge-stroll away from the mountain town of Marshall. Funded in part by the arts council, an abandoned old high school there had become studios for twenty-six working artists. As a direct result, galleries, small businesses, more art studios, and tourism had sprung up. "I saw all of these great things that were happening," Hill says. He thought: "Art is transforming this community. Why can't it do the same thing in Kinston?"

Collector

Stephen Hill

KINSTON

Kinston entrepreneur and civic leader Stephen Hill is an avid collector of art, a booster of art, and a believer in the power of art to change lives.

His contributions to the cultural life and economic success of his hometown—including his purchase and restoration of fifty-four former mill houses for artists to live in and his work to create a specially zoned arts and cultural district—have been widely recognized, earning him the Esse Quam Videri Award from Visit NC and the Designlife Award from NC State's College of Design, among many others.

The impact he's proudest of making, though, might be the least visible to a visitor. It's the way that art education supported by the smART Kinston program he spearheaded is changing the lives of the city's children. Because the artists who are given the opportunity to live in the subsidized, refurbished houses of Kinston's Arts and Cultural District agree to work in the city's schools, Kinston kids have the opportunity to learn from working artists.

At Rochelle Middle School, artist Catherine Hart "let [students] express themselves, and it made such a difference," Hill says. "They could voice themselves and be proud of their school and themselves. Art has just changed that school. I want to continue to do that." □

Stephen Hill at Rochelle Middle School with (left to right) K'ala Green, Ja'maya Outlaw, Rochelle Middle School principal Felicia Solomon, and Madysen Hawkins.

Tobacco was good to this once-prosperous city in its heyday; so were cotton and textiles. The decline of all three, coupled with devastating flooding from Hurricanes Hazel, Fran, and Floyd, took a major toll. But the beginnings of a real renaissance have taken place over the last decade, spurred largely by art and the creative businesses that have sprung up around it, and they're not all Hill's. Celebrity chef Vivian Howard's The Chef and the Farmer restaurant—and the blockbuster PBS documentary series it generated, *A Chef's Life*—attracts diners from all over the world.

"It's amazing what art does for a community as an economic driver," Hill says, standing on the rooftop of the O'Neil, the luxury boutique hotel he created in the hull of Kinston's long-dormant Farmers & Merchants Bank building. It's just one of a half-dozen historic downtown buildings he's revitalized in his hometown. Over his shoulder stands Mother Earth Brewing (the nation's first LEED-Gold certified brewery, with local art on every wall and on every label), which he founded with his son-in-law Robert Mooring in 2008. His Mother Earth Motor Lodge and Red Room music venue are around the corner. Behind him stand the seven earthcast tobacco barn silhouettes that make up *Flue* by artist Thomas Sayre, which Hill, smART Kinston, and the North Carolina Arts Council commissioned to honor the city's tobacco heritage.

ROCKY MOUNT, WILSON, AND ENFIELD

Other Eastern North Carolina towns with similar boom-bust histories have also found new life through art. Wilson, once known as "the world's greatest tobacco market," was brought to kinetic life in 2017 when thirty massive whirligigs made by outsider artist Vollis Simpson were moved from his farmland in nearby Lucama to the mostly derelict city center. The North Carolina Arts Council, the National Endowment for the Arts, and private foundations provided funding.

Wilson resident Henry Walston, original chair of the Whirligig Park and Museum, says the idea for the park centered on "creative placemaking," a conscious plan to create an artistic vehicle for economic development. Between its opening and the summer of 2021, Walston estimates the project has sparked more than $50 million in downtown investment and the creation of several new businesses, art galleries, studios, restaurants, bars, and apartment buildings. Whirligig Station, a tobacco warehouse turned apartment building across the street from the whirligigs, rented its ninety-two loftlike units almost immediately upon opening.

The project "really has taken flight," Walston says. He and his wife, Betty Lou, have devoted endless time, energy, and constant warm hospitality not only to the park but to Wilson's creative community, which is booming. "I always said, when we were working on the park, that we could be a poster child for creative placemaking for a town our size," Walston says. "And we are achieving that status."

Artist Elizabeth Laul Healey says it's a vision shared by the creative community. "There's a great communal sense of building back the downtown, a sense of common cause," says. "And all of us artists, especially, support each other."

Celebrated photographer Burk Uzzle may be the best known among them, but he's not alone. California native Healey bought a defunct Amoco gas station across the street from the whirligigs and spent two years turning it into a studio/gallery to make and show her art, which includes larger-than-life figures she calls "Iconostars." Every day, Healey says, she asks gallery visitors where they're from. "Forty percent of them are from out of state," she says. "From Florida to Maine, every single week."

They've read about the whirligigs online or in the *Wall Street Journal* or *Washington Post*. Because Wilson is just about exactly halfway between Florida and New York, it's a good place to make a stop. "I'm getting a lot of that overflow," she says. So are the other artists and shops, including the Selkie, a next-door store and gallery owned by North Carolina artist Amanda Duncan and featuring work of many others.

Barbara White is another beneficiary of and contributor to the scene. The Chapel Hill artist was so taken with the town's emerging creative community and its stock of interesting, affordable old buildings that she bought a handsome but badly neglected 1920s-era corner building a few blocks from the whirligigs and painstakingly renovated it into The Edge, a combination gallery-studio-loft-apartment. The result is so impressive—and the idea of moving just thirty-five minutes east of Raleigh so easy to imagine—that several artists have followed her lead, says Allen Thomas Jr., a lifelong Wilson resident, art collector, and civic leader. "Barb was kind of the beginning." Now, he says, downtown is becoming an at-

Nautilus (from rePiano)

Jeff Bell
WILSON

Jeff Bell takes apart everyday objects, like pianos or rocking chairs, and turns the pieces into sculptures that tell new stories.

When a piece of a dismantled 1911 piano reminded him of the shape of the *Nautilus*, Captain Nemo's submarine in the 1954 Disney film *20,000 Leagues under the Sea*, he was inspired to make his own version, which became *Nautilus (from rePiano)*.

A similar imaginative leap resulted in *ReNautilus*, an elegant and intricate work of art he built for the 21C Hotel in Durham. It started with research, beginning with the year 1937, the year the hotel's Art Deco building was built. He learned that the Golden Gate Bridge was also completed that year, that the Hindenburg Blimp exploded, and that a beautifully illustrated edition of Jules Verne's *20,000 Leagues under the Seas* was published. The resulting work expresses the adventure, duality, and danger shared by all of them.

It was a far cry from Bell's earliest days as an undergraduate artist at UNC Wilmington focused on painting. An internship with a local artist, Al Frega, first opened Bell's eyes to the potential of sculpture, and of art as a profession. "I grew up in Goldsboro and had limited experience being around the arts, even though I always made things and drew, but I didn't really comprehend that a person could be a working artist."

These days he's doing just that, and also involved in the world of art, broadly speaking, as the executive director of the Vollis Simpson Whirligig Park in Wilson.

Meantime, his own work continues to evolve. Most recently, he's focused on letting creativity—not laborious planning—guide his creations. He's doing that by zeroing in on what's most important about a particular work. "I've narrowed my focus in order to become more creative," he says. □

Nautilus (from rePiano), by Jeff Bell, 2014. 60 × 72 × 40 in. Wood and metal. Photograph by J. Caldwell.

tractive place to live. "It's booming. It's legit." He credits the city of Wilson for responding enthusiastically, welcoming artists and helping them find grants to help with restoration.

Also to thank: the new 20,000-square-foot Wilson Arts Center. In a formerly boarded-up downtown department store, the center now boasts 5,000 feet of gallery space that's drawing artists and audiences from around the state. An exhibit of photographs from Thomas's own important collection of photography launched the space in May 2021. "It's a lot of fun" to share some of the work he has collected over thirty-five years, he says; it's also the fourth or fifth time he's shared pieces from his 600-work collection with the city for exhibits over the last twenty-five years.

Art contagion is visible on any short stroll around the Whirligig Park. Just a few blocks away, on the corner of Barnes and Tarboro Streets, a circa 1900 building originally built as a saloon is now an art gallery. Around the corner is the Eyes on Main Street Wilson photo gallery, headquarters for the international street photography festival that began here in 2015 and that every year fills downtown storefronts, walls, and buildings with 100 large-scale photographs of street life around the world taken by photographers from dozens of countries. The festival, described as "bringing the world to Wilson," has been covered in *Vogue Italia* and other international publications, and also runs a National Endowment for the Arts–funded visiting artist program that hosts photographers from all over the world in Wilson year-round. The Walstons have hosted several and now count photographers from Lithuania, Mexico, England, and Australia as friends.

All of this art is a magnet for people and for the businesses that follow. As many as half a dozen restaurants and bars popped up in the space of a year or two, Thomas says—Casita Brewing across from the whirligigs is a hot spot, and so is Bill's Grill a few blocks away on Nash—and others are in the works. "Art and food are really reviving our downtown," he says.

Barton art gallery at Barton College might not be new, but it's getting new attention and energy from Wilson's art boom. The gallery regularly showcases the work of North Carolina artists, including a recent exhibition by William Paul Thomas, and hosts a regular rotation of prestigious artists-in-residence. Its undergraduate art program is considered one of the best small-college art programs in the state.

The formula so successful in Wilson—art plus place equals prosperity—is inspiring to even a small town like Enfield, founded in 1740, about halfway between Rocky Mount and Roanoke Rapids, population 2,500, with a downtown that reflects its late-1800s tobacco-and-peanuts prosperity. Art has brought life to its quiet streets in recent years, mostly thanks to artist Myra Wirtz and her husband, Andrew Wirtz. The couple moved to Enfield from New Jersey in the 2010s, bought a historic house, scooped up the one across the street to serve as her studio and as an art gallery, and bought the town's historic Masonic Temple to turn into a performing arts center. In 2019, artist and curator Charles Philip Brooks helped them put together an exhibit of contemporary art by North Carolinians (including Chieko Murasugi and Ashlynn Browning) in a onetime department store building in downtown Enfield. The show was the first of a series.

Not far away, in the long-beleaguered former textile and tobacco hub of Rocky Mount, a 135,000-square-foot nineteenth-century site of the Imperial Tobacco Company of Great Britain and Ireland was transformed in 2005 into the Imperial Centre for the Arts & Sciences, home to art galleries, community art programs, a children's museum, a planetarium, and community theater. Among the many programs

Collectors

Allen Thomas Jr. and Marjorie Hodges

WILSON AND RALEIGH

Allen Thomas Jr.'s collection of art by living artists, many of them photographers, is widely known for its breadth, depth, and quality. Amassed over the past thirty-five years, the 600-piece-plus collection—one of the state's largest individual collections—has been exhibited in major solo shows at museums including the North Carolina Museum of Art, Raleigh's Contemporary Art Museum, Winston-Salem's SECCA, and the Blowing Rock Art & History Museum, and has been loaned to more than fifty exhibitions worldwide. The collection was bigger before he started giving it away—125 works to the NCMA and others to the Turchin Center for the Visual Arts in Boone and the Taubman Museum of Art in Roanoke, Virginia, among others.

"I don't have a good eye,'" says the Wilson resident. "I just buy what I like." What he likes are works of art that "people can't walk by without a response," he says. "I'm less into pretty things and more interested in strong images."

His business partner, Marjorie Hodges, a longtime art professional and art consultant who has held senior roles at the NCMA and Raleigh's CAM, is similarly inclined. The Raleigh resident's collection includes painting, sculpture, photography, and textiles from the region and beyond. "I think of art collecting as a practice," she says. "I thoroughly enjoy the process of online viewing, studio visits, art fair hopping, and connecting with artists wherever I am in the world. Living and learning from art are two of life's greatest pleasures."

Hodges has lived in North Carolina for twenty years and says the wealth of artistic talent here is more impressive than ever. "Some of the most innovative and compelling artists I know live and work in the state, and are increasingly participating in the global art market," she says. "Talent abounds."

In 2020, Hodges and Thomas, the two longtime friends, launched an online platform and marketplace for artists and collectors called Artsuite. With a roster of artists including many North Carolinians (for example, Barbara Campbell Thomas, Beverly McIver, Donald Martiny, Jeff Bell, Peter Glenn Oakley, Thomas Sayre, and William Paul Thomas), Artsuite's goal is to demystify art, advocate for artists, and connect people with art. □

Business partners Allen Thomas Jr. and Marjorie Hodges at Thomas's Wilson house in front of his large-scale painting by Raleigh artist Corey Mason.

sponsored by the city-owned Centre are three annual national juried exhibitions. The Sculpture Salmagundi is a national outdoor sculpture competition that results in a yearlong exhibition; the Juried Art Show is a national multimedia exhibit installed every year from May to August; and Handcrafted focuses on art made of craft materials for a show that's up from January to April every year.

Not long after the Imperial Centre was complete, plans to turn the derelict 150-acre campus of Rocky

Mount Mills into a work-play-live complex began to take form. The 1818 cotton mill and adjacent sixty-odd mill houses on the Tar River had been abandoned for nearly twenty years before the Capitol Broadcasting Company, owned by the Jim Goodmon family, bought and overhauled the campus, turning it into apartments, office space, event space, a tiny-house boutique hotel, a beer brewery incubator, and dozens of rehabbed mill houses that were fully occupied in no time.

Bessie Coleman

Richard D. Wilson Jr.

GREENVILLE

Bessie Coleman, by Richard D. Wilson Jr., 2015. 24 × 26 in. Pastel on archival sanded pastel paper. Courtesy of Richard Wilson.

"When I first started painting, I wanted to put out positive Black images, because whenever I looked at the paper I always saw the negative side," says Greenville artist Richard D. Wilson Jr. "Especially with children, if they keep seeing that stuff, they will believe that's all they are, or that's all they can be. I wanted to put out there what I knew was true about my community."

He also wanted—and wants—to educate people, and not just children, about the proud legacy of Black heroes from the past. In his *Shadow* series of paintings and pastels, Wilson depicts young Black children standing beneath ("in the shadow of") these people, among them Barack Obama, Muhammad Ali, and Michael Jordan. He also paints lesser-known heroes like Lee Elder, the first Black

American to play in the Masters golf tournament; Jack Johnson, the first Black American world heavyweight boxing champion; and Bessie Coleman, the first Black American woman and first Native American to hold a pilot license.

"All through school, I heard about Amelia Earhart, but I never heard about Bessie Coleman," Wilson says. Born in 1892 to a family of Texas sharecroppers, Coleman "taught herself a whole new language, French, because she was denied [flight school] education in America," Wilson says. With the encouragement of Robert Abbott, the publisher of the *Chicago Defender* newspaper (whose chronicles of her achievements and untimely death provide the background of Wilson's painting), Coleman earned her pilot's license in France.

For most of his life, Wilson has been driven to draw and paint people who inspire him. Growing up in Robersonville, NC, he was encouraged by his artist father (who worked as a clothing-pattern maker, sign painter, and math teacher) to develop his talent. For many years, Wilson juggled a burning desire to paint with school and a series of unfulfilling jobs that paid the bills. The difficult decision to paint full time has led to a more successful career than he could have dreamed, he says today.

"I've never looked back." □

EITHERWAY

Gabrielle Duggan

GREENVILLE

Gabrielle Duggan was pursuing a fashion degree when she realized that her longtime fascination with textiles could become a wellspring for an art career instead.

Textiles had captivated her since she was a child. "I remember staring at the back of my mom's couch, saying 'How did that thread go under and then over, and then under that other thread, thousands of times? How did this happen? How is this something nobody's talking about?'"

When she learned how fabric was woven, "it felt like the foundation of the universe . . . it showed me that the world is held together in suspension . . . by this potential energy of intertwining and twisting things so that they are not allowed to fall apart. You build up this tension, and then lock it in place."

This interest has only grown through her art, inspiring her to spin giant, magnificent spiderwebs; to weave intricate woven images; to bind geometric steel shapes with gossamer threads and suspend them in midair. These category-defying creations refer to the tension between opposing forces, the ways those forces define each other and the dynamics between them. They are beautiful and abstract and also "reflect social, political, and historical implications of power," Duggan says.

At NC State, where she earned a master's degree in art and design, Duggan explored what she describes as the "deep-rooted connection between looms and computers,

and technology and coding, and of course patterns, and math, and music." Since then, her work has been exhibited extensively in solo and group shows across the Southeast. Currently a professor at East Carolina University's School of Art and Design, Duggan has created several public works and won many grants and awards.

Her interest in fiber and its potential seems inexhaustible. Duggan grew her own cotton at one point and spun her own yarn, "working from the fiber up," as she says. "I just dug in. I wanted to understand everything."

In the fall of 2020, she created a 300-foot-long temporary woven outdoor installation called EITHERWAY across an "off-shoot of an off-shoot" of the Tar River on Tuscarora land outside Greenville. She used simple crochet techniques to connect strands of a surplus ballistics textile called DSM Dyneema across the water from her floating kayak below, spelling out the word "eitherway" as she went. It stretched and dipped and fell in parts. The word, even in its imperfection, reflected for her the resilience required by the pandemic, the sentiment that "we will survive this either way."

Water is an important part of this piece and many others, she says. "There's a lot that I'm fascinated about with water," especially the phenomenon of surface tension. The place where a mass of air meets a mass of water, she says, is particularly interesting: "It is not a finite point." □

EITHERWAY, by Gabrielle Duggan, 2020. 40 × 300 ft. Surplus ballistics textile. Photograph by Kevin Cirnitski. Courtesy of Gabrielle Duggan.

Farther toward the coast, the city of Greenville has long known the importance of art. With a growing reputation as one of Eastern North Carolina's cultural hubs, Greenville is home to East Carolina University and its respected art department and MFA program, founded by Leo Jenkins, the school's sixth chancellor.

It's also the site of the Greenville Museum of Art, founded in 1960 by a local group determined to foment and support the arts in the East. Spurred on by Greenville native Robert Lee Humber, who'd been instrumental in founding the North Carolina Museum of Art, the group was inspired to create their own arts appreciation society. That society went on to purchase a historic home and found a museum. Today it boasts the world's largest public collection of watercolors by American artist Andrew Wyeth, a significant collection of paintings and prints by contemporary artist Jasper Johns, an important collection of North Carolina pottery, a gallery devoted to the work of beloved twentieth-century North Carolina artists Francis Speight and Sarah Blakeslee, and a survey of American art from colonial times to the present.

Another notable small museum is farther south in Fayetteville, where Methodist University's David McCune International Art Gallery has exhibited the works of Rembrandt, Andy Warhol, Marc Chagall, and Pablo Picasso, in addition to that of students and North Carolina artists.

About forty-five minutes farther south in Robeson County is Pembroke, considered the cultural, social, and political home of the Lumbee Tribe. Recognized as North Carolina's largest tribe with more than 55,000 members, the Lumbee have long-standing art traditions celebrated by contemporary artists like Alisha Locklear Monroe and by UNC Pembroke's Museum of the Southeast American Indian, which was founded in 1979 with a mandate not only to preserve Native American culture in the region but also to "encourage American Indian artists and crafts persons."

The art department at the university has a similar mission. Billed as the only state-supported university in the United States created "by American Indians for American Indians," UNC Pembroke was founded in 1887 near the banks of the Lumber River, which gives the tribe its name.

Eighty miles farther is Wilmington, home to the Cameron Art Museum, widely considered the premier museum in Eastern North Carolina and one of the most important small museums in the state. Housed in an elegant 2002 building designed by groundbreaking architect Charles Gwathmey on land donated by the family of Bruce B. Cameron and Louise Wells Cameron, the museum, originally founded by volunteers in 1962, has a commitment to showcasing and collecting the work of North Carolina artists as well as artists from around the world.

Outdoors alone, the Cameron has one of the state's few public sculptures by Mel Chin, a work called *The Structure of Things Given and Held*, a Vollis Simpson whirligig, and ceramic tile seating by famed Little Switzerland–based ceramic artist and painter Tom Spleth. Other important North Carolina artists in the museum's collection include renowned Asheville-born, New York–based painter Donald Sultan, Penland-area basket maker Billie Ruth Sidduth, and deceased groundbreaking twentieth-century artists including Romare Bearden, Minnie Evans, and Maud Gatewood. In 2021, the Cameron Art Museum installed a significant exhibition of the works of Davidson's Elizabeth Bradford, and commissioned Durham's Stephen Hayes to create a life-size bronze monument to the United States Colored Troops who fought in the 1865 Civil War battle of Forks Road on the site of the museum.

"We have no parent institution, we are not state supported. We are community owned," says Director Anne Brennan, a Wilmington native. Philanthropic support from the Bruce Barclay Cameron Foundation has always been a cornerstone, she says, but additional philanthropic support is vital. "We're built by the community and sustained by the community," Brennan says. "It keeps us, without question, accountable to our region. We have got to be in service, we have got to listen and act, or we're gone."

The fact that the Cameron is in fact alive and well speaks highly for Wilmington's legacy as a place that has long valued the importance of art in many forms. The city has its own symphony, the Wilmington Symphony Orchestra, and boasts one of the country's few NPR member stations that are wholly community supported, unaffiliated with a college, university, or public television station.

There's a frontier spirit behind these community-generated institutions, Brennan points out. "Wilm-

Waiting for Author

Cynthia Bickley-Green

GREENVILLE

Cynthia Bickley-Green's art mines the worlds of neurobiology, geometry, and the visual phenomena that reside within the eye. "The visual field is not necessarily out there," she says. "It's in your head."

Examples that fascinate her include floaters, or slowly-drifting shapes that move across a plain of vision, or the swiftly moving, tiny white dots that sometimes whiz past before a bright blue sky.

"I feel that elements of entoptic imagery show up in . . . painting from abstract artists," she says. Bickley-Green spent a couple of years painting "what you see when your eyes are closed," but the resultant black paintings didn't work as well as she'd hoped. So she took the entoptic forms and combined them with the hues she'd explored as a member of the Washington Color School group of painters in the late 1960s and early 1970s.

Her work is also inspired by sound. "Our visual perception is linked to our hearing," she says. Birdsong is something she sees in her mind's eye; music, is, too. "You can listen to some loud, loud music, and close your eyes, and then listen to some classical music and close your eyes. And I think that you will find you'll see a different movement in that . . . sparkly field you see when you close your eyes."

Bickley-Green's paintings have been shown in more than 100 exhibitions and are in public collections including those at the Corcoran Gallery of Art in Washington, DC, and American University. She is the author of the book *Art Elements: Biological, Global, and Interdisciplinary Foundations*, has been a professor of art at East Carolina University for nearly thirty years, and has received grants from the National Endowment for the Humanities and the NC Arts Council. □

Waiting for Author, by Cynthia Bickley-Green, 2014. 42 × 42 in. Acrylic paint on canvas. Courtesy of Cynthia Bickley-Green.

ington is more like an island, the way the Cape Fear River and the ocean define our spit of land. And so it's really made our thinking [similar to] the way island people think," she says. Until I-40 was extended to the coast in 1990, "We were cut off from other parts of the state, and that makes us very scrappy people," Brennan says. "On islands, whatever it is that you choose, that you value, that you want for your community, you've got to make it yourself. And I hope that we don't lose that." The resources that spirit has built are important factors for the area's economic health and growth, she points out. "It's not just proximity to the beach" that inspires people to move to Wilmington, she says; it's proximity to culture, too.

If North Carolina's coast provides an inspiring setting for the appreciation of art, it's also ideal for the making of it, Brennan points out. "This has always been a great place for artists to work. It's been relatively low cost," she says, and "the muse is here."

Chemical between Us

Alisha Locklear Monroe

LUMBERTON

Artist Alisha Locklear Monroe, who works primarily in acrylic, describes herself as a proud member of the Lumbee Tribe. She shares her cultural history not only through her work, which uses abstraction and symbolism to reflect her individuality as well as her heritage, but also as museum educator at the Museum of the Southeast American Indian at UNC Pembroke.

"I love advocating and representing," she says. In 2012, Locklear Monroe cofounded the River Roots Arts Guild to promote fellow artists from Robeson County, the home of the Lumbee people and the place she was born and raised. She also launched a seasonal marketplace for local artists.

As devoted as she is to promoting her fellow Lumbee artists and preserving the Lumbee culture, Locklear Monroe says when it comes to her own art, she wants it to stand on its merits.

"I want to be valued as an artist first, and then for my message," she says. She's been drawing since she was a child but didn't think of herself as an artist until she was a freshman at UNC Pembroke and was encouraged to paint from her own imagination, rather than replicate something she'd seen before. "That was the moment that turned things around for me," she says.

Today her art reflects both her imagination and her culture. "I'm committed to being a keeper of history and a communicator of that history," she says. Many of her fellow local artists feel the same way, she says, but it can be difficult to get that message out. "Our Native artists, especially in Robeson County, feel like we don't have an outlet, a place or a platform, outside of the museum [of the Southeast American Indian]," she says. "It can be really frustrating. . . . Native southeastern art is lost to many people."

For her part, Locklear Monroe has found a wider audience, exhibiting her work throughout the state, including at the Center for the Study of the American South. She has won the award for Best in Contemporary Artists at the NC Tribes Unity Conference, and her work is in the collections of UNC Greensboro and UNC Pembroke. □

Chemical between Us, by Alisha Locklear Monroe, 2018. 24 × 36 in. Acrylic. Courtesy of Alisha Locklear Monroe.

February Window

Sue Sneddon

SHALLOTTE

When Sue Sneddon was a child growing up in Boston and wanted to understand how nature worked, she drew it. For the rest of her life, nature's mysteries had her in their thrall, and art remained her response. Sneddon spoke at length about her art and her life in an April 2021 interview. She died in January 2022.

Her paintings of sea and land and the places they join are reverential. Photographically realistic but also dreamlike, they capture the light as tangibly as they do the water; somehow, temperature, smell, and sound are in there, too. She began *February Window* on Emerald Isle in 2018, at a moment when "Emerald Isle did its emerald green thing, right out[side] my bay window of the third floor of the cottage. And I just sat there and did one pastel after another, and took notes."

She took notes and sketched on Emerald Isle for more than forty years, several weeks at a time, usually around the September equinox. She chose it as the ideal place to paint after traveling to every coastal town in North Carolina in the late 1970s. The state had originally lured her during childhood car trips down to the beaches of South Carolina with her family. "I had to be awake when we went through North Carolina," she says, "because the tobacco barns fascinated me, the fields and the trees." The feeling never left her, and as an adult, she made the state her home.

Her fall stays on Emerald Isle were pilgrimages. Because it sits on the east-west-oriented barrier island of Bogue Banks, Emerald Isle's beaches face south. "The light on the water, especially for an East Coast beach, is just different," Sneddon said. "You get to see the sunrise and the sunset standing in the same spot, especially at equinoxes."

For many years she made the trip from her longtime home in Durham; in recent years she lived in the equally beautiful Shallotte but still made the trip to Emerald Isle every September to paint and to teach.

"It's the beginning of a creative process for me," she says. That process was highlighted by an annual sunset swim in Bogue Sound on the date of the equinox. "I go in, usually up to my chin . . . and physically watch the season change." Instead of setting over the mainland, the sun at that moment goes down behind the bridge to Emerald Isle, on its journey toward the ocean side. "It's a physical feeling. We're moving to another place in the sun."

Her ability to capture that visceral connection and communicate it in paint is what fueled her career. Sneddon had solo exhibitions at galleries throughout North Carolina and South Carolina, including fourteen over twenty-five years at Durham's Craven Allen Gallery. □

February Window, by Sue Sneddon, 2018. 30 × 24 in. Oil. From the collection of Donna Nicholas, Edinboro, Pennsylvania. Courtesy of Sue Sneddon.

It would be hard not to find that muse along the inland shores or on the unspoiled beaches of North Carolina's Outer Banks. On nearby Bald Head Island, artists from all over the world vie every year for residencies at the island's No Boundaries International Art Colony. Housed in three historic cottages that overlook the state's southernmost coast, this rotating group gathers to make art and exchange cultures and ideas for two weeks every November. While they're there, they create pieces for a group exhibition at the Wilma W. Daniels Gallery on the campus of Cape Fear Community College and collaborate with the UNC Wilmington Department of Art and other organizations.

Another group welcoming artists from all over is Pocosin Arts School of Fine Craft, which stands on the banks of the Scuppernong River just before it reaches Albemarle Sound.

Founded by Feather Phillips in 1994 to "connect culture to the environment through the arts," Pocosin plays an important and growing role in the art ecosystem of Eastern North Carolina. As Penland does in the mountains, Pocosin on the coast offers year-round artist residencies, workshops, classes for all ages, and a teaching studio and art gallery in nearby Columbia, which carries a large number of paintings by Sue Sneddon.

The school began a significant campus expansion in 2021 to build a gallery and expand studios for more and bigger classes and workshops, reflecting a growing number of artists in the region and more people of all ages interested in art and art education. No doubt it also reflects the "muse" that the Cameron Art Museum's Anne Brennan cites: the area's unique coastal beauty, an inspiration as old as time.

It was enough to make a painter out of North Carolina writer and Wilmington resident Clyde Edgerton, the author of ten novels and a Guggenheim Fellow known fondly as "North Carolina's Mark Twain."

"When you're in a place near the ocean, or perhaps the mountains, something happens that is so deep you can't understand it," Edgerton says. "A lot of people want to go one step beyond just appreciating it . . . to creating something that resembles what you see, so that you can maybe get at what you feel."

CHRISTINA LORENA WEISNER

KITTY HAWK

Christina Lorena Weisner assembles her sculptures, zips up her wetsuit, and wades into the March-cold waters of Kitty Hawk Sound. It's barely six A.M., the sun's not fully up, the air's barely forty degrees, and the art she's wrangling is bigger than she is, but Weisner takes it all in stride. The next thing you know, she's glided fifty yards from shore and her art's floating all around her.

It makes sense that this sculptor and installation artist is at home in the natural world, that she's unperturbed by cold water, early mornings, and ungainly physical feats. A former competitive swimmer and beach lifeguard, her work taps into the intersection between people, objects, and the natural environment, illuminating the way we live within the world and the way the world lives with us. The largest of the

three sculptures bobbing beside her on this morning is the one she attached to her outrigger kayak and towed 275 miles down the Eno and Neuse Rivers and through the Ocracoke Inlet in 2019, recording audio-visual information and environmental data (including a panther sighting) along the way.

A Richmond, Virginia, native, Weisner says she can trace the beginnings of her work as an artist to a job she had with Nag's Head Ocean Rescue in her early twenties. When she wasn't saving swimmers, she stared out at the ocean for ten hours a day. "I would watch the sun move across the sky, the moon come up, and you just become very aware of these bigger processes . . . these large-scale movements, like the waves coming over from the coast of Africa . . . that we're not often aware of."

Other little-seen influences in her work come from her wide-ranging education (which includes an MFA and separate undergraduate degrees in both world studies and fine arts), and include the relativity of time, the metamorphic properties of natural elements like silica, and "the interesting phenomenology" of Tibetan Buddhism, including its appreciation of the "fullness and emptiness of forms."

From her home in Kitty Hawk, Weisner rides a bike or runs along the beach every day to note its transformations. "It's the same beach, but it's completely different, the water color, the form of the waves, the temperature of the wind." Sometimes she finds objects to incorporate into sculpture as she goes, like the discarded beach chairs that form the two smaller works with her in the water on this day.

Waves and wavelengths—audio, seismic, and light—all inspire her. The Nördlinger Reis meteor impact crater in Germany was the subject of sculpture and installation art she created with the Fulbright Grant she was awarded in 2013; she used seismometers to record earthquakes as part of a Mint Museum installation in 2018.

Her approach with every subject, she says, is to embrace what she doesn't know, and to let her new knowledge as well as her material—which is sometimes composed of found objects and scientific instruments and sometimes is the landscape itself—to guide her.

"I'm still a process-oriented artist," she says, one focused on "openness to material and play, not taking my work too seriously . . . and not being too pigeonholed." She thrives when she can employ all her senses in the making of her art, especially work that involves nature. "It's super important for me to use my body to understand the landscape," she says. "I ride my bike, and run, and hike, and walk the whole thing as a way to understand the space. I always think about embodying kinesthetic experience, learning through moving your body . . . and it's magnificent." ∎

BEN KNIGHT

DEEP RUN

Ben Knight is not an abstract expressionist. His paintings, he says, are not abstractions. They are realistic: "realistic expressions of emotion."

These range, clearly, from rough and furious to placid, from inward and muddy to bright and engaging. "The effect that my day has on my emotions, and how I choose color . . . is very intuitive, but also very intentional," he says. "I'm drawn to certain colors in certain moments on certain paintings at certain times because they have an emotional context."

Knight credits renowned abstract painter Larry Poons, with whom he studied in New York, with "setting something loose for me," for helping him tap into the fluidity and intuition he already had as an athlete. As it did on the basketball court, it began on the canvas with speed. "He'd say faster, faster, more color, faster. It allowed me to use my instinct and my eye."

Now an established working artist, Knight has time to explore color, technique, and tempo in the modernist studio behind his family house that sits deep in a Deep Run soy field.

It's all a long way away from Knight's Chicago childhood. A self-described "jock" growing up, he

but he doesn't think of them that way. They're more like siblings, relatives that share some, but not all, essential DNA. The first time Knight took on multiple paintings at once was with three works called *The Hand*, *The Heart*, and *The Eye*, a reference to daily Jewish prayer, "connecting hand, head, and heart three times a day to center and focus yourself."

Other titles for his work come to him less directly, applied to various paintings after the fact. A wall of his studio is covered with these Sharpie-scrawled phrases and words: "Uncooked Soul" and "Light Don't Think" are checked off. Among the dozens still up for grabs are "How's It Tasting" and "Chopped Liver Man."

If the titles are haphazard, the painting is not. An underlying geometry is at work, scaffolding what he describes as a "thick and chaotic" surface. It's a practice inspired in part by the abstract expressionist Barnett Newman, who described painters as "choreographer[s] of space" and used a vertical band of color he called a "zip" to focus and unite a canvas and its viewer.

Knight is also fascinated by the interaction between viewer and canvas, by what a painting becomes when it is beheld. "As I work now: what is the intent or the emotion that I am leaving for people to feel? That's the next thing I'm very interested in. Combining this idea of putting emotions on something through color, and then documenting what viewers think." ▪

was also immersed in art thanks to his artist grandmother, who picked him up after school every day and took him to the classes she taught at Lake Forest College and other schools. But it wasn't until Knight became an English major in college that he tapped into his own creativity. Jack Kerouac's *The Subterraneans*, in particular, made a huge impact. "I got very into that book because I loved the spontaneity of it," he says. "And I think more than anything, that really influenced how I make art."

He does it in fast bursts, three or four canvases at a time on his working wall, and paints them simultaneously, most often with a wood-handled Venetian plaster knife he found in a local hardware store. Occasionally, he uses a brush. The result is series-like,

FACING
Ben Knight in a field
outside his Deep Run
house and studio.

ABOVE
Strong Minded Fools, by Ben Knight,
2019. 48 × 48 in. High resin acrylic
on canvas. Courtesy of Ben Knight.

SEPTEMBER KRUEGER

With subtle, watery colors, delicate stitching, layered images, and the unexpected juxtaposition of organic and designed shapes and lines, September Krueger's intricate quilts and silk paintings celebrate nature, birds and plants, and the environments they share. They are the work of an artist with a deep, sensory appreciation for her subject and her medium.

From an early age, Krueger loved to draw. She studied textiles as an undergraduate in Philadelphia with the idea of becoming a fashion designer, but her graduate work at East Carolina University opened her eyes to the potential of textiles as an artistic medium, and inspired her to "develop layers of information on woven cloth."

A kimono she made at ECU was the turning point. She was on familiar ground when it came to the sewing and structure of the garment but found herself pulled in a new direction with the fabric itself and the stories it told. "All of the motifs were of cloth that had been batiked, and all of the batiked imagery... related to religion, which comes up a lot in thinking about myself and my family." From that point forward, function took a back seat. "Wearable became less and less important."

She uses silk and other fluid fabrics in her work today, enabling her to "build up the surface in so many ways, almost like a collage artist," often repeating motifs like a small bird or a leaf. These also show up in her finely wrought woodblock prints, which mine much of the same territory of the natural world.

September Krueger with one of her quilts in Wilmington.

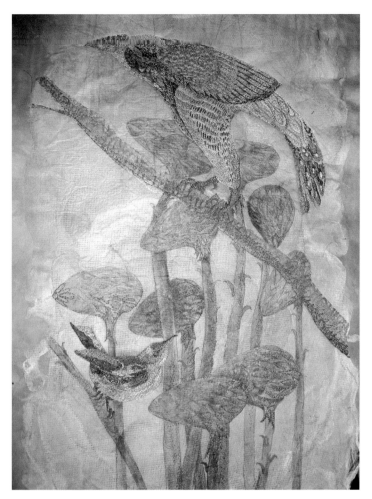

Krueger's community focus goes beyond Wilmington. In Kinston, she and Anne Brennan (the executive director of the Cameron Art Museum and a fellow artist) designed tile mosaics—inspired by the work of iconic North Carolina artist Romare Bearden, and created together with the young women of a community development organization called The Gate—for installation in Kinston Music Park.

And her work as head of the art department at Southeastern Community College takes her to Whiteville, North Carolina, regularly. "I found a community immediately here in Wilmington, between the university and the community college. I found that there are outstanding artists in our community college system. And I also met people who were at different stages of life and were going back to study and figure out what they might want to do. . . . Art connects them all." ∎

Central to Krueger's artistic calling, she says, is an instinct to share it, and use it to build community. As director of lifelong learning at Wilmington's Cameron Art Museum, one of her central goals is to open the museum's offerings to new populations. Paradoxically, she says the pandemic might have helped with that effort, because people who might not have taken themselves to the museum in person to see an exhibit in ordinary times have been compelled to visit virtually. "Having shifted some of those barriers that people may have had about the museum" as a place that might seem intimidating, "it would be wonderful" to have them become a regular part of its educational and artistic community, she says.

The Wren Would Be King, by September Krueger, 2010. 12 × 19 in. Machine embroidery on silk paper. Photograph by Curtis Krueger.

BURK UZZLE

WILSON

When Burk Uzzle opens the double red doors of his studio, gallery, archive, and home in downtown Wilson, North Carolina, it's impossible not to feel as if you're being let in on a wonderful secret. It's not just the realization that one of America's most accomplished and celebrated photographers is right here, living at the center of this former tobacco town, or the surprise of seeing his iconic historic photographs and striking new ones on the walls.

It's that he is so disarmingly informal, so charming in his flat cap, wool vest, and jeans, so willing at eighty-one to leap upon a waist-high platform for a portrait, to frankly discuss his inspirations, to dig into his archives, to describe at length the ways he uses lighting and state-of-the-art digital tools to refine the large-format photographs he prints himself, "making it feel dimensional and tactile."

"It's all theater, so I usually pump the theater," he says. "I'm not a believer in very quiet, passive, uninteresting colors." Or days. Uzzle rises at 4:30 every morning to ride his mountain bike outside for an hour, "getting a hell of a workout and looking for

unforgettable photo of the young couple embracing under a blanket at sunrise amid a sea of bedraggled bohemian concert-goers on the cover of the *Woodstock* album is his. The indelible picture of Martin Luther King Jr. in his casket, published on the cover of *Newsweek* magazine the week he died, is also his. Mentored by Henri Cartier-Bresson and a longtime member of famed photographers' cooperative Magnum Photos, Uzzle for decades captured memorable American images of urban and rural life: politicians, farmers, athletes; parades, peace protests, places.

He's a master of composition and of light—he says his best lessons have come from museum paintings—but his photographs have something bigger at their core. In his words, "a big heart and a strong eye."

An expansive frame of reference doesn't hurt. "Photography's more like music than it is like anything else," he says. "Good photographs are an opera. The ones that really work have a narrative, as an opera does, and then they have the structure, the drama, the visual, and the music. A combination of a lot of different components that come together to make a form."

After decades spent around the world making operatic photographs, Uzzle made the decision in 2007 to return to his home state to document life here now. Some of that work takes the form of the images he spots on those early-morning rides—landscapes that tell stories, everyday people going about their lives—and much of it takes the form of portraits he creates to draw attention to the remarkable individuals he encounters and the difficult issues that grip him most: gun violence, rural poverty, racial justice, and Black lives.

"It's taken me a lifetime to understand how important it is to do this," he says. "When I die, this will be my signature work in North Carolina." ∎

pictures at the same time," before returning home for yoga. After that, he works "like a sumbitch in the studio all day."

The conjoined city buildings he's made his own had previous lives as a car dealership and a coffin factory. It's doubtful they've ever seen industry quite like Uzzle's.

A staff photographer for the *News & Observer* at eighteen, Raleigh-born Uzzle became *Life* magazine's youngest-ever staff photographer at twenty-three and made his name documenting the youth culture and civil rights movements of the 1960s. That

ROBERT B. DANCE

KINSTON

When Robert B. Dance was a high school student in Kentucky, he had his own radio program. He was talkative and outgoing, interviewed musical guests, played the guitar and ukulele, sang, and thought he might have a full-fledged career in the music industry. Instead he became one of the nation's leading nautical artists, his work exhibited in the Great Hall of the Smithsonian, at the North Carolina Museum of Art, and in the nation's foremost gallery for marine art, the Maritime Gallery at Mystic Seaport. Dance's painting of the Cape Hatteras lighthouse became the nation's first National Park stamp; our state's own Maritime Museum opened with an exhibition of his works; and twenty years ago, our Southeastern Center for Contemporary Art installed a twenty-year retrospective on his career.

He says it was a love of art and the natural world that combined to turn his life's focus to painting. A courtly gentleman, Dance describes himself these days as quiet and introspective, but he welcomes visitors to his Kinston home studio with the energy of the teenage radio personality he once was,

answering questions not only about his paintings—there's a finely detailed painting of a set of breaking waves at Atlantic Beach recently begun on his easel—but about the many, many other artifacts, bits of nature, and things he's made by hand that crowd the space, each of them a physical representation of his lifelong fascination with nature, animals, boats, and music.

There are the models he makes to paint from, like a small Maine lobster boat, and the birds he paints and even flies, including a radio controlled, full-scale red-tailed hawk. There's the ukulele he's making by hand (arthritis in his left hand has made it hard for him to play chords these days, so he "thought it would be interesting to try lutherie"). There are the pieces of nature he's brought inside to replicate, including an extraordinary collection of feathers.

"I love birds," he says. "I wish I could fly." He holds a little lifelike hummingbird he carved by hand. "I would sit outside in the yard with a flower in my mouth, leaning up against the house, hold this [little hummingbird], and wait, and wait, and wait to see if a hummingbird would come and try to get honey out of the flower in my mouth. I'll tell you: artists are crazy."

Born in Tokyo in 1934, the son of an American tobacco executive, Dance says that he soaked up the artistic sensibility of the Japanese from an early age.

FACING
Robert Dance in his
Kinston home studio.

ABOVE
Cape Lookout Morning, by
Robert Dance. Courtesy
of Robert Dance.

EASTERN NORTH CAROLINA   245

"The first thing I ever painted was a watercolor of an iris when I was six years old," he says, "and I've been painting ever since." He would go on to study illustration, creating woodcuts for *Playboy* magazine, and working as an illustrator and designer for books and companies that ranged from furniture makers to General Electric and Wachovia Bank.

A great admirer of the painters Thomas Eakins and Andrew Wyeth, Dance found his life's true calling when he began to paint the natural world. It's no small feat to begin a new work: He immerses himself fully, taking months at a time to perfect each canvas, putting himself fully into the painting, feeling the wind, or the shade of the passing cloud, or the nervous-making swell of a wave, hearing the birdsong, smelling the brine.

"Nothing is more vital or interesting than nature," he says. At eighty-six, his enthusiasm only grows. "I have a childlike curiosity, still. I constantly learn." ■

JACK SAYLOR

ATLANTIC BEACH

Every evening, Jack Saylor walks a couple of blocks from his airy studio to the wide sands of Atlantic Beach. There, he sets up his easel to paint the sunset. He's making studies, mostly, sketches of the sea, of the sky, of the light. It's "a means to an end," a way to "inform the environment for my still life work in the studio." Unless he's outdoors, painting the world around him, he says, he misses out on "the breeze, the magic, the whole spectrum of the color of the sky when the sun finally sets."

Known widely for meticulous, photo-realistic landscapes and seascapes of the North Carolina coast, Saylor has recently shifted his focus to still life, but his passion for the sea, for the play of light and color, and for the expansive natural world continues to fuel his work. Back in the studio, when he zeroes in on the velvety petals of a rose, a single reflective drop of water on a curl of lemon rind, or the transparency of a leaf, he's channeling that energy. He's also tapping into techniques he learned as a young man in Spain and Italy, where he studied the works of Italian Renaissance painters and those of the Dutch seventeenth century. Those painters' ability to harness light and dimension, to refine detail and honor beauty, made a lasting impression. And so as Saylor paints, his brushstrokes disappear, the two-dimensionality of his canvas disappears, color, light and shadow dominate, and everything but his subject falls away.

Jack Saylor painting the afternoon sun on Atlantic Beach.

247

*Ode to Victory,
Grace and Glory,*
by Jack Saylor,
2021. 24 × 28 in.
Oil on canvas.
Photograph by
Scott Taylor.

Doing this kind of work in the home state he loves was his ultimate goal as a young Barton College graduate from Wilson, North Carolina, traveling through Europe as a product designer for Sarreid, a US importer. Working with artists and craftsmen and learning as he went, Saylor longed to put it all to use closer to home.

Moving back to the North Carolina coast, he saw the ocean and coast with new eyes and abilities, and made his name depicting it. In 2007, when the state of North Carolina sought a still life painter to depict artifacts recovered from the shipwreck thought to be the pirate Blackbeard's *Queen Anne's Revenge* as part of its QAR Shipwreck Project, it was the ultimate opportunity. Saylor filled a large canvas with the pirate's flag, cannon, cannon balls, and other objects. *Under the Black Flag* is hyperreal and historically accurate but manages to hint at the pirate's mendacious legacy.

The shift from the kinetic world outside to the still life within represents a natural progression. He recalls a critic early on describing his landscapes as similar to still lifes. "It got me thinking: That is how I approach things. I wasn't necessarily an atmospheric painter," or one focused on perspective or depth of field. Instead, "I went in and painted this tree, that tree, this tree—individually. And that's the way you approach a still life. They're objects. A gathering of objects." His seascapes were the same: "That wave. . . . And then the foam. And then the next one. And the next one. As if it were a still life. It's the way it works for me, for what I'm after." ∎

ANN CONNER

WILMINGTON

Bright colors, sharp shapes, and irregular, organic material combine to make Ann Conner's woodcut prints unmistakable. Look at me, her work commands, enjoy me. Then try to figure me out.

Large-scale and distinctive, her art may appear simple from a distance, but reveals its rigor and complexity as a viewer approaches. The wood grain of these pieces is swirling, unpredictable, "seductive," as she says; so is its marriage with her opaque, precision marks, her saturated, man-made hues.

These pieces have pride of place on the walls of the Ackland Museum in Chapel Hill, the Cameron in Wilmington, and the North Carolina Museum of Art in Raleigh. They're also in more than fifty other major museum and corporate collections across the country.

Originally a painter focused on portraiture and the natural world—Conner earned an MFA in painting at UNC–Chapel Hill and taught studio art at UNC Wilmington, serving as department chair—Conner says she became "disenchanted with reality" after a number of years and decided to focus her imagination on abstraction. She was inspired to explore it through woodcut prints after becoming fascinated by the antique Japanese woodcuts of Kabuki actors on her mother's wall.

Woodblock printing, Conner points out, is the oldest form of printmaking. She carves her blocks here, four or five days a week, in a contemporary sunsoaked Wilmington studio, using oak and other woods like walnut, elm, cherry, or birch and a hightech Japanese-made Automach power chisel. Before

Ann Conner with two of her woodcut prints in her Wilmington studio.

she carves, Conner does extensive drawings with a technical pen called a Rapidograph, designed for engineers and architects to produce sharp, consistent lines. She also uses templates to delineate some of her shapes. The carving itself is tiring work, best completed no more than a few hours at a stretch. An air mattress and sleeping bag in the back allow her to grab a quick nap before picking up her chisel again.

"If I had another aspiration, it would be to be a sculptor." Her prints, she points out, "are very sculptural. That's kind of where I'm coming from." But she's not interested in stepping away from her current work to do it: "It's just the wood cut. I'm just so into it."

"There's no hidden meaning," she says of the stars, flowers, loops, and swirls that fill her picture planes. "They are just pure abstractions." She finds her templates in unlikely places like Lowe's or Williams Sonoma, where she picks up cookie cutters and other objects. She knows she's got a good one when they "just click."

Then Conner takes pains to match these designs and shapes to the particular grain of wood before her. But most important is color. "Color is paramount," she says. "Certain colors don't go with certain designs."

Once she's completed her carvings—a process that can take a few months—she sends them to a specialty printer in Austin, Texas. She travels there to meet her work and then begins the proofing process, experimenting with colors. The hand-printing process itself is laborious and time consuming, sometimes taking two to three people working together to complete.

And then she's back to her studio and to the inspiration that comes to her not through the beautiful coastal scenery outside her door, or through music, or current events, or her own interior thoughts, but through the work itself.

"It's concentration. I feel like you have to generate your own inspiration, through materials, materiality, and that goes for colors, and ink and wood. I think materiality is something I have come to appreciate from the minimalists: Donald Judd, Joel Shapiro. The materiality of what you're working with is important." ∎

AFTERWORD

Before I began this book, I knew there was a great story to tell about the visual art of North Carolina. As a journalist, I had written, assigned, and edited countless feature stories about the artists of the Triangle. I was amazed by the depth of their talent and the ecosystem that supported them, knew their numbers reached across the state, and couldn't wait to start reporting.

But when I did, I quickly learned that what I'd glimpsed was only the shimmering surface of a much deeper ocean. This story was bigger, more diverse, and more relevant than I'd imagined. It had a complex history, was populated with fascinating characters, and illustrated something important about our state, about its pride, creativity, and ingenuity, its self-awareness, and its ability to manifest what it valued most.

I couldn't believe my luck. A huge story lay before me, one that had been told in bits and pieces but never comprehensively, a story about North Carolina's visual art of all kinds, all mediums, and all

messages. A representative sample of the extraordinary diversity of art and artists who live and work in North Carolina. How and where and why was all of this art happening here? When did it all start? Who was making it, and what they were making?

I knew the book had to have excellent original photography and was delighted when the talented Lissa Gotwals agreed to photograph the artists and collectors for the project. I also knew that the photography wouldn't be possible without meaningful philanthropic support. I was honored and immensely grateful when the Lewis R. Holding Fund agreed to become the book's presenting sponsor. I was also thrilled when the North Carolina Community Foundation, the Thomas S. Kenan III Foundation, the Mary Duke Biddle Foundation, the A. J. Fletcher Foundation, First Citizens Bank, the Josephus Daniels Charitable Fund, and patron of the arts Jim Romano agreed to become supporting sponsors.

And then COVID hit.

How was I going to interview artists? Not to mention curators, collectors, museum directors, gallerists? How was Lissa going to photograph them? As with many aspects of the pandemic, this forced pause had a silver lining, though that wasn't immediately apparent.

I knew I had to find a different way to work. Because I didn't have the luxury of connecting the dots of this story over an extended period of time, in-person interview by in-person interview, I had to hone my focus at the outset and conduct my initial interviews over the phone—something I usually avoid, as face-to-face conversations can be so much more nuanced, informative, and engaging.

As it turned out, these many initial telephone interviews were a godsend. When it came time to speak in person, I had compiled a far more comprehensive understanding of the statewide community of art than I otherwise would have.

That understanding was the culmination of more than 200 interviews with artists, gallerists, curators, collectors, art entrepreneurs, and museum professionals across our wide state. These generous people told me everything that books could not. How was art being made here today, and who was making it? Every person had a valuable perspective on who, and what, and how. How did it all evolve? Many had seen it happen firsthand. Whom else should I speak with? The list grew, and grew, and grew.

When the strictest COVID lockdowns had begun to lift and Lissa and I started traveling the state to visit artist studios, continuing precautions made it practical for my in-person follow-up interviews to take place at the same time as Lissa's photo shoots. I think we were both surprised at how enriching this turned out to be.

"Due to COVID, there was much more double-duty work to do," Lissa says. "I really enjoyed toggling back and forth between the photos and the interviews. Often, I am not fortunate enough to have so much understanding and information about the people I get to photograph. It both helped inform some of my choices photographically and made for a more fulfilling experience all around."

The same was true for my reporting. As we together explored studios with artists, moved things around to set up for photographs, and chatted informally before any actual interviewing took place, I was able to learn more about each artist as a human being than I would have in a typical sit-down format.

As our work drew to a close, Lissa and I were both wistful—it has been an extraordinary, meaningful adventure—and we were also determined. Determined to keep telling stories about art and artists, determined to keep shining a spotlight on the extraordinary people making North Carolina one of the most dynamic, creative, and exciting places there is.

ACKNOWLEDGMENTS

This book would not have been possible without the generosity of countless kind, thoughtful, and knowledgeable people in every corner of our state. In true North Carolina fashion, these artists, curators, collectors, museum directors, gallerists, and civic leaders opened their doors and invited me into their homes and offices and museums and galleries and studios; they drove me around their cities and towns and regions and showed me their art; they endured my COVID-era requests for Zoom interviews and long phone calls; they let me ask them far too many questions. Most of all, they trusted me with their stories.

When the time came to photograph the artists and collectors among them, these wonderful people welcomed the talented photographer Lissa Gotwals in, too, and let us take over their entire mornings and afternoons with photo shoots and more interviews. In every encounter was the sense, spoken and felt, that the endeavor was meaningful because the art of North Carolina needs to be known and acknowledged, that it is important culturally, economically, and spiritually, and that it deserves celebration.

That same understanding was shared by the generous donors who believed in this project from the beginning. Their contributions underwrote Lissa Gotwals's photographs and helped these stories come alive. These donors include the book's lead sponsor, the Lewis R. Holding Fund, as well as a remarkable group of supporting sponsors including the North Carolina Community Foundation, the Thomas S. Kenan III Foundation, the Mary Duke Biddle Foundation, the A. J. Fletcher Foundation, First Citizens Bank, the Josephus Daniels Charitable Fund, and patron of the arts Jim Romano. I am greatly honored by their support and deeply grateful to each of them for providing it.

I am also grateful to the following people for their kindness, time, expertise, and support in the course of reporting and writing this book: Carmen Ames, Mia Hall, Libba Evans, Frank and Julia Daniels, Peter Bristow, Jim Goodmon, Mimi O'Brien, Damon Circosta, Thomas S. Kenan III, Jennifer Tolle Whiteside, Pamela Myers, Allison Perkins, Stephen and Erin McDonald, Andrew and Harper McDonald, Becca Roberts and Dan Hartman, Steve Roberts, Marjorie Hodges, Allen Thomas Jr., Chandra Johnson, Valerie Hillings, Linda Dougherty, Kristin Replogle, Beth Moye, Van Nolintha, Orage Quarles III, Joyce Fitzpatrick, Joel Fleishman, David Woronoff, Henry and Betty Lou Walston, Johnny Burleson, David Brody, Marion Church, the late Joe Rowand, Melissa Peden, Carole Anders, Jo Cresimore, Renee Snyderman, Mina Levin, and the Watauga Club.

Thanks also to the late Ola Maie Foushee (1931–1999) for her independently published 1972 book, *Art in North Carolina: Episodes and Developments, 1585-1970*, which provided important historical context. So did *Two Hundred Years of the Visual Arts in North Carolina*, a 1976 publication of the North Carolina Museum of Art.

A huge thank you also to my editor, Lucas Church, for championing and shepherding this book from concept and proposal to manuscript and completion, and to my smart, capable, and enthusiastic research assistant Tennessee Woodiel for making sure the details didn't get lost in the shuffle.

When Lindsay Starr became art director of UNC Press just in time to design this book, I knew that she was great at what she did and that I was lucky. Now that I know she is also patient, kind, and not just good at what she does but beautifully talented, lucky seems a paltry word. Thank you, Lindsay.

Of course I knew I was lucky when Lissa Gotwals agreed to be the photographer for this book. We had worked on many stories together at *Walter* magazine, and I considered her the most talented photojournalist I knew, particularly adept at capturing creative people in their environments. The results are more beautiful than I could have imagined, and it was wonderful to become such great traveling companions, friends, and collaborators. Thank you, Lissa.

I would also especially like to thank Lawrence J. Wheeler for sharing his extensive knowledge, for his unflagging support, and for his generous friendship, all of which are exhibited most recently in the foreword of this book. Thank you so much, Larry.

I would like to thank my parents, Judith and Stephen McDonald, for exposing me to art from a very young age, for showing me the power of curiosity, for encouraging me to follow my instincts, and for believing in me. Thanks also to my children, Regan, Hale, and Cecilia Roberts, for their sustained and ardent enthusiasm and curiosity about this book. I can only hope that they feel as supported, loved, and encouraged by their parents as I have always felt by mine. And finally, I would like to thank my husband, Lee, for making sure all of that is true for our children, and for always doing the same thing for me.

INDEX